COLLECTED ECONOMIC ESSAYS

Volume 7

REPORTS ON TAXATION I

COLLECTED ECONOMIC ESSAYS
by Nicholas Kaldor

The Level of Company Taxation

108. With regard to the amount of taxation to be levied on companies we understand from the Board that it would require a flat-rate tax of 40 per cent. to produce approximately the same revenue from company taxation as the existing income tax and profit taxes yield at present. Since the marginal rate of tax on company profits is at present a minimum of $47\frac{1}{2}$ per cent. (i.e., the income tax of 45 per cent., and the profits tax at the undistributed rate of $2\frac{1}{2}$ per cent.) and would amount to 53 per cent. if the profits tax were charged at a uniform rate, the change in the method of charging the tax levied on companies would alone have considerable advantages. By reducing the marginal rates of tax it would reduce the incentives to wasteful expenditures (such as advertising or entertaining) afforded by the fact that almost one-half of any additional outlay by companies is financed out of the consequential saving of taxation.

109. We believe, however, that with the introduction of a capital gains tax there is a case for reducing the total burden of company taxation below the present level since the ultimate incidence of the taxes paid by companies is likely to fall on the owners of equity shares (taken collectively) in much the same way as the taxes on capital gains. We therefore recommend that as the revenue from the capital gains tax begins to flow in (which for reasons explained would not happen immediately) the rates of company taxation should be pari passu reduced, until the corporation profits tax is reduced to the rate of $33\frac{1}{3}$ per cent. which we consider to be the rate ultimately appropriate at the present general level of taxation.

110. We base this conclusion on the following considerations:—
(i) that the saving which takes the form of capital appreciation whilst taxed at a flat rate, and not at a progressive rate, should be taxed at much the same average rate at which it would have been taxed had it formed part of the ordinary income of shareholders; (ii) that owing to the concentration in the ownership of property, and particularly of equity capital, that rate is likely to be appreciably higher than the standard rate of income tax; (iii) the company tax is a tax on capital appreciation (on equity owners taken as a group) in the same way as the tax on realised

capital gains, the difference being mainly one of timing—whilst the company tax is paid, in a sense, in advance of the accrual of capital appreciation, the capital gains tax would typically be paid some years after it; (iv) the weight of the tax on company profits, when considered as an indirect tax on capital appreciation, depends not only on the rate of the tax but on the proportion of company profits that are distributed or retained. Thus a tax of $33\frac{1}{3}$ per cent. on company profits is equivalent to a tax of 43 per cent. on company savings, assuming one-third of net profit after tax is distributed and two-thirds retained; to a tax of 50 per cent. on savings, assuming one-half of net profits to be distributed; and to a tax of 60 per cent., if two-thirds of the net profits are distributed.

111. It is reasonable to assume that with the removal of the discriminatory profits tax on dividend distributions companies would ultimately tend to distribute around 50 per cent. of their net earnings (instead of the present 28 per cent.) which would mean, on the basis of the 1953 income of companies and a $33\frac{1}{3}$ per cent. corporation profits tax, a gross dividend distribution (subject to income tax) of around £m1,1000, in place of the 1953 figure of (around) £m600. On this basis the total tax charge on capital appreciation would amount to $72\frac{1}{2}$ per cent. (i.e., 50 per cent. in the form of a tax on company savings and 45 per cent. on the remaining 50 per cent. in the form of the capital gains tax) or 14s. 6d. in the £. This is not an unreasonable figure, if it is remembered that it is a tax on the marginal income of share-holders and that a part of the tax will, in the typical case, be paid with a considerable delay.

112. It may be relevant to point out that in the United States the corporation profits tax, levied at the rate of 52 per cent., alone takes some 70 per cent. of the undistributed corporate profits (i.e., 23 out of 33 billion dollars in 1953) on top of which is the capital gains tax of 25 per cent. which, if added on analogous assumptions, would imply a further tax of $7\frac{1}{2}$ per cent., so that the total tax on capital appreciation comes out at $77\frac{1}{2}$ per cent. We regard it as a considerable merit of our proposals as against the system in force in the United States—both from the point of view of equity and economic effects—that the part of the charge which

would be levied on companies is considerably lower (a rate of 33⅓ as against 52 per cent.) and the part which would be levied directly on individuals is considerably higher (45 as against 25 per cent.) than in the United States.

IV. THE DIFFERENCE IN CONCEPTION BETWEEN SCHEDULE D INCOME AND SCHEDULE E INCOME

113. In the case of an office or employment, the income to be charged is the actual receipt in the year less only those expenses which are incurred "wholly, exclusively and necessarily in the performance of the . . . duties" of the office or employment. If the same conception were applied to the profits of trading, professional or vocational activities only such expenses would be deductible as could be shown to have been necessarily and inevitably involved in producing the receipts of the year in question. This would be the case if the range of deductible expenses were limited to the materials and fuel consumed and labour actually expended on the production of those goods and services the sales proceeds of which constituted those receipts. The original method of computing profits for tax purposes must have been something akin to this. But in the course of years, and under the influence of accountancy principles, this conception was more and more departed from. The departure took form (i) in the permission given to a trader to anticipate unrealised future losses by valuing his stock at current market values if that is below cost; (ii) in the allowance given for capital expenditure; (iii) in reckoning as current expenditure all such expenses as can be said to be "wholly and exclusively" laid out for the purpose of the trade or profession (whilst not constituting the purchase or a capital asset of some kind)—even if they have no traceable connection with the receipts of the current year, or if the Majority's recommendation as to the Schedule D expenses rule were adopted—were not even incurred "for the purpose of earning the profits", present or future.[1] Advertising and enter-

Para. 128.

tainment are typical examples of expenses incurred for building up the goodwill of a business, which, though fully chargeable against the current year's receipts, are frequently linked with receipts, if at all, only through the enhancement of future rather than current earnings.

114. Nothing similar to this would be a deductible expense under Schedule E. The wage or salary earner cannot charge as expenses the cost of entertaining his present or his potential future employers even though the expense might be "wholly and exclusively" incurred with a view to securing for himself a better job. Nor could he charge the cost of training or education (whether in the form of a capital allowance or as current expenses) or the annual wear-and-tear to his physical earning powers. For all these reasons "income" under Schedule E is not analogous to the net profit under Schedule D; it is more analogous to some conception of a "gross profit" of trade, before the deduction either of depreciation or of all those other expenses which are not directly associated with the current receipts from trading activity. The Commission has heard much evidence of the practical effect of this difference in conception in representations from those professions (such as the acting profession) whose members are assessed under both Schedules.[1]

115. While these liberal provisions concerning deductible expenses under Schedule D may in some cases contribute to a fairer allocation of taxation as between one trader and another, they do so at the expense of producing unfairness as between traders and other taxpayers. At the same time they make the tax system a far more difficult one to administer, since with the inclusion of all such indirect items it becomes increasingly difficult to draw a sharp line of distinction between business expenses and personal expenses. It must also be borne in mind that expenses which are not directly or closely associated with the trading operations are voluntary on the part of the traders. Whether they are incurred or not, or the scale on which they are incurred, depends very largely on the net cost to the trader, who is bound to take the consequential saving of taxation into consideration. When taxation is at all heavy, the system of allowing the deduction of

---

[1] Cf. in particular Minutes of Evidence, Day 19.

such indirect expenses incurred "in the course of trade" amounts to a very considerable subsidy from the Exchequer on outlays of doubtful value, which it might not have been worth the trader's while to incur at all in the absence of taxation.

116. It is well known that income taxation can distort normal economic behaviour through its disincentive effects on work, saving, and the assumption of risks. It is less well known that analogous distortions are caused through the stimulus the tax system provides to expenditure of various kinds which are not necessary or inevitable concomitants of producing the receipts against which they are set off. In the case of expenditure on unavoidable items no such subsidy is involved precisely because the trading receipts are directly dependent on them. The outlays on fuel, wages, materials, etc., are not affected by the tax provisions; and if deductible expenses were confined to the range of such unavoidable expenses, the distortions caused by the tax system on the allocation of the community's resources would be minimised.

117. For all these reasons a tax on trading receipts less unavoidable expenses (which comes broadly to the same thing as a tax on the value of the net output, as defined for the Census of Production, *less* outlay on wages, salaries, interest and rents) would be fairer and less arbitrary in its incidence than the present type of tax on profits; it would be a far simpler tax to administer; and since the tax base would be so much broader, it would make it possible to effect a reduction in the rates of taxation. Nevertheless we feel that it would be futile to advocate for immediate adoption such a radical departure from the existing practice so long as the profits taxation of other countries remains on the present basis. For our traders engaged in overseas trade might be put at a competitive disadvantage if they were not allowed to treat as deductible expenses selling and promotional outlays of various kinds which qualify for tax deduction in the case of their overseas trade competitors. We also feel that, while the above line of reasoning argues in favour of the exclusion of capital allowances as well as indirect expenses, the case for such allowances is so strong on purely economic grounds that we would not support their abolition.

118. We would like to put on record, however, our view that the United Kingdom should press, through the United Nations or other international bodies, for the adoption of binding international conventions concerning the principles to be followed in the taxation of trading profits which would make it possible to proceed towards a more rational, effective and equitable system of profits taxation than any one country would be able to adopt acting in isolation.

119. If the present difference of conception between Schedule D and Schedule E income cannot be removed by narrowing the range of deductible expenses under Schedule D the question arises whether it can be narrowed or eliminated by widening the range of deductible expenses under Schedule E. This problem has two aspects: one is whether it would be possible, or desirable, to introduce a system of capital allowances with respect to the expenditure incurred in professional and vocational training, etc. (this question affects all earnings from work, including those taxed under Schedule D); the other is whether the expenses rule under Schedule E could or should be assimilated to that of Schedule D.

120. While we are in agreement with the view of the 1920 Royal Commission that allowing for the wastage of the source of income in the case of material assets and ignoring the wastage of the human element in income production leads to "grave inequalities as between different classes of income",[1] we are of the opinion that it would not be practicable to introduce a system of capital allowances with regard to the investment in the human person. Claims for such allowances would have to be confined to such expenditures as serve the purpose of, and are incurred solely with a view to, increasing the earning capacity of the individual. From an administrative point of view it would be very difficult, if not impossible, to devise a scheme that would be effectively confined to expenditures of this kind. Professional training is not necessarily distinct from general education; and even in the case of outlays upon specialised training and education, it would be impossible to establish whether the outlay incurred served solely economic purposes or whether it included an element of personal expenditure.

[1] Cmd. 615, paras. 181 and 182.

121. Similarly we do not believe that the present difference in conception could be effectively removed by rephrasing the expenses rule under Schedule E so as to make it more akin to that of Schedule D. As the Majority explain,[1] the strict character of this rule, originally introduced in the Income Tax Act of 1853, has attracted a great deal of criticism over the last thirty years, not only from interested taxpayers, but from judicial quarters. Nevertheless we are satisfied—after studying the evidence submitted to the Commission by the Board—that this "very narrow and strict rule" is a powerful safeguard of good administration. For once expenses voluntarily incurred by an employee in connection with his duties are admitted as permissible deductions from his income it becomes very difficult to draw a clear line of distinction between such expenses and personal expenses; or between expenses reasonably incurred and those that are not reasonably incurred. Moreover the range of expenses recognised as "reasonably incurred" in any particular class of employment would inevitably become steadily wider in the course of years. As Mr. Justice Rowlatt once said, "there would be no end to it".[2]

122. In our view if the Schedule E expenses rule were relaxed the same problems which now beset Schedule D assessment would be reproduced in the case of Schedule E—new avenues would be opened for tax avoidance and for disputes between the Revenue and the taxpayer—with little, if any, net gain in equity as between one Schedule E taxpayer and another. We do not support therefore the change in wording of the Schedule E expenses rule recommended by the Majority,[3] a change which in our opinion does not go nearly far enough to remove the difference between the two conceptions of income, and might yet have the effect of relaxing the existing rule sufficiently to make the tax more difficult to administer and more arbitrary in its incidence.

123. In the circumstances we feel that the only remedy is to recognise the difference of conception openly and to compensate for it, in a broad manner, through a differentiation in the rates of taxation imposed. Such differentiation already exists in our

---

[1] Paras. 129–131.
[2] Simpson v. Tate, (1925), 9 T.C. 314, at p. 318.
[3] Para. 140.

tax system in the form of earned income relief. It remains to examine whether the existing limitations in the application of that relief, according to size or type of income, are those most in accord with the requirements of equity.

124. The differentiation in our tax system between "earned" and "unearned" incomes was introduced in 1907. As the 1920 Royal Commission put it, "Although recognition of the principle was a long time in coming, the demand for it is practically as old as the tax itself".[1] The basis of that demand, voiced both before the 1851 and 1861 Select Committees on the Income Tax, lay in the consideration that incomes from work are precarious and in consequence a man who depends on income earned by his personal efforts and exertions needs to make provision out of his income for retirement or ill-health in a way in which a man who derives his income from property does not. The relief introduced in 1907 was so framed as to give effect to this principle. The relief extended to the profits of unincorporated business as well as the profits of professional and vocational activity, and to incomes derived from offices and employment. It has been limited, however, since its initial introduction, to an income of £2,000 (at the present time £2,025). The logic behind this limitation was that, in the case of unincorporated businesses the profit is the joint outcome of the capital employed and of personal exertion; that the part played by capital is larger, the more extensive and remunerative the business; and therefore it is more practical and equitable to treat profits in excess of a certain amount as being in the nature of income from investment rather than income from personal exertion. There was never any logical reason, however, why any such upper limit should be applied in the case of incomes wholly derived from personal exertion such as those assessed under Schedule E; or in the case of those profits where the role played by material capital in the production of the income is small—as in the profits of professional and vocational activity assessed under Case II of Schedule D. It is possible that when Parliament originally introduced these provisions in 1907 it was believed that incomes in excess of £2,000 a year were largely to be found among traders assessed under Case I of Schedule D; and no great

[1] Cmd. 651, para. 106.

injustice would therefore result if the principles considered valid in the case of that particular type of income were applied to all other forms of income as well. No such supposition is valid today.

125. Since earned income relief was first introduced, the need for a person depending on earned income to save up for retirement has been further recognised in superannuation relief. The present scope of this relief will be greatly extended if the recommendations of the second Tucker Committee, endorsed by the present Royal Commission (and referred to in paragraph 191 below), are adopted. This means, in the opinion of the Majority, that "the tax system differentiates in favour of earned income by two unrelated instruments and there is the danger that the same factor will be weighed twice over".[1] We believe, however (as we said previously in paragraph 30 of a Reservation to the Second Report of the Commission[2]), that whatever the historical reason for the introduction of the differentiation may have been, "precariousness" should not be regarded as the sole, or even the most important, reason for maintaining a difference in treatment as between incomes from work and incomes from property. In our view there is a strong case for making some allowance—even though the cost cannot be precise—for the real cost involved in working as opposed to owning property: for recognising the fact that in performing work, a man, in the words of Adam Smith, "must always lay down the same portion of his ease, his liberty, and his happiness". Secondly, the monetary cost of acquiring knowledge and skill, which is fully analogous to the capital cost of plant and equipment, receives no recognition in the tax system, unless it be found in earned income relief. Finally, there is the important difference in the treatment of expenses which differentiates, not incomes from work and incomes from property as such, but incomes assessed under Schedule E as against incomes assessed under Schedule D.

126. We believe that the existing provisions with regard to earned income relief could be so amended as to give recognition to the above considerations.

127. In the first place the existing upper limit to earned income relief, justified by reference to the "mixed" character of incomes

---

[1] Para. 70. [2] Cmd. 9105, pp. 72 et seq.

jointly derived from work and property, should be limited to incomes which are truly "mixed" in this way—i.e., to profits of trade assessed under Case I of Schedule D. The principle has clearly no application in the case of incomes assessed under Schedule E. We believe also that in the case of the profits derived from a profession or vocation the element of property in the production of the income is small, and is being reduced or eliminated by the gradual disappearance of the custom of buying and selling practices. In our view therefore it would be more equitable to treat incomes assessed under Case II of Schedule D as incomes that are fully earned and to which therefore the idea of an upper limit does not apply.

128. The difference in treatment between Schedule D and Schedule E incomes, due to the differences in the treatment of expenses, to some extent cuts across the distinction between incomes from work and incomes from property. We do not believe, however, that equity would be better served by introducing a second instrument of differentiation; we believe on the contrary that with suitable provisions the existing instrument of earned income relief could take care of differences of both kinds.

129. We therefore recommend:

(i) Earned income relief should be available to all incomes assessed under Schedule E without any upper income limit.

(ii) In the case of individuals and partnerships who derive their income from a profession or vocation assessed under Case II of Schedule D, the earned income relief should be available without any upper limit, but should only be available to those taxpayers who at their own option are willing to be assessed on their profits under the Schedule E expenses rule.

(iii) In the case of unincorporated businesses assessed under Case I, earned income relief should only be available up to the limits recommended in paragraph 220 of the Second Report of the Royal Commission,[1] and should only be available to taxpayers who at their own option are willing to be assessed on their profits under the Schedule E expenses rule.

[1] Cmd. 9105.

(iv) Taxpayers exercising the option mentioned in (ii) and (iii) would not be able to claim such expenses as are (*a*) not of a capital nature; (*b*) not directly and inevitably involved in earning the profits of the current year. This would exclude all those payments laid out exclusively for the purposes of trade but not spent on items actually consumed in the current year's trading operations (the items actually so consumed being reckoned when stocks are valued on actual cost), or not manifestly necessary for conducting these operations.

130. We believe that these arrangements would recognise the inherent differences between incomes from work and incomes from property adequately; and, at the same time distinguish between, and treat accordingly, those who do and those who do not derive considerable advantage from the more liberal expenses rule applicable to Schedule D.

131. The Board estimate the cost of the unlimited extension of earned income relief in the case of Schedule E incomes at £m10–£m12. The yield of the withdrawal of earned income from Schedule D taxpayers will depend on the number of taxpayers who exercise the option. Assuming that two-thirds of those assessed under Case II of Schedule D and one-third of those assessed under Case I exercise the option the yield—taking into account the cost of the unlimited extension of the relief for Case II—is estimated at £m25–£m30. It is impossible to say what extra income would be brought into charge as a result of restricting expenses for Schedule D taxpayers who exercise the option. It would obviously be less than the relief thereby secured and if it averaged half of such relief the yield might be of the order of £m10–£m15. On these assumptions therefore the net effect of the above recommendations would be a net gain in revenue of the order of £m25–£m40.

V. PARTICULAR ISSUES CONCERNING THE TAXATION OF
PROFITS

132. While we are in favour of a reduction in the weight of taxation imposed on company profits as part of a wider reform, we are strongly opposed to the process whereby the concept of taxable profits is being whittled down by the granting of new concessions and exemptions of various kinds. As we pointed out in paragraphs 24–28, unless arguments and claims for such concessions are judged in the light of a guiding conception of taxable income, the tax base is likely to be whittled down in a capricious manner with serious consequences for the general equity of the tax system.

133. Demands for further concessions and exemptions of this character put before the Royal Commission related to the complete exemption of overseas profits from taxation; extensions in the kind of foreign taxes that should qualify for double tax relief; the introduction of new kinds of capital allowances, such as the mining depletion allowance; the introduction of some scheme of replacement cost depreciation for fixed assets, and the L.I.F.O.[1] method of valuation for current assets. The Commission have resisted these claims in some cases (such as replacement cost depreciation); remained formally undecided in others (such as the general exemption of overseas profits from taxation, though the Majority recommend a scheme in this connection which could amount to much the same thing in practice); in yet others they partially acknowledge the claim for extended concessions (as in the field of double taxation relief); while the Majority concede the case as regards stock valuation and the mining depletion allowance.

134. In the following sections our treatment will be confined to cases where we consider that existing concessions ought to be restricted or withdrawn, and cases where we dissent from the Majority's recommendations or on which our assent is conditional on the acceptance of other recommendations made in this Memorandum.

---

[1] "Last in, first out", as compared with F.I.F.O., "first in, first out", referred to on pp. 78–79.

A. RELIEF FOR LOSSES

135. At present if a taxpayer assessed under Case I or Case II of Schedule D has an excess of deductible expenses over receipts he is regarded as showing a "loss" which may be offset against income from any other source in the current year or the following year, or carried forward indefinitely as an offset against future income from the same source.

136. This situation, in which an income may be regarded as negative, can only arise in cases where taxable income is arrived at by deducting the costs of producing that income from gross receipts. Thus since no costs of production (such as expenditure on acquiring personal skill and other training, or on efforts to obtain new employment etc.) are recognised in the case of wage or salary earners assessed under Schedule E, income from an office or employment could be zero but could never in practice be negative. A property owner who does not carry on a business may sustain capital losses as a result of a failure of investment but these are not recognised as negative income. In the case of an owner of real property who has an excess of repair or maintenance costs over the income arising from his property, the excess is not recognised (except that in the case of a landlord of agricultural property the maintenance costs and depreciation allowances on new buildings and works may be set off against his agricultural income generally).

137. As the Majority point out, "if the idea of a loss of income involves that more money has been spent than has been received on income account during the period, the balance has in some sense been found out of capital: and to set the loss against taxable income, current or future, is to allow the depletion of capital to be made good at the expense of taxable income".[1] In our view the very notion that the taxable income derived from a positive source (such as a trade, profession or employment—we are not here considering interest on a debt which is derived from a negative source) could be treated as a negative or minus quantity is incongruous within the framework of a tax system which ignores capital gains and losses in the determination of taxable income.

[1] Para. 486.

Thus, at present, a trader assessed under Schedule D enjoys an anomalous privilege in that losses of a capital nature are regarded as diminishing his taxable income, though gains of a capital nature are ignored for tax purposes.

138. If capital gains and losses were brought within the tax charge generally, on the lines we recommend in paragraph 65, the notion of allowing losses of a capital nature as a deduction from taxable income would no longer in itself be anomalous. But the present definition of a trading loss by no means corresponds with the definition of a capital loss for purposes of a tax on capital gains—the definition required to give expression to the comprehensive conception of income described in paragraphs 5–7. A trading loss at present is looked upon as a loss on current (not capital) account; but since various expenditures of a capital nature have come to be treated as deductions from current receipts in the calculation of taxable income under Schedule D, a trading loss on current account may result when certain capital outlays in a period exceed net current receipts, or even when certain capital outlays of a past period exceed net current receipts.

139. It is possible to regard capital allowances as covering current expenses of production in so far as they are annual allowances for the wear and tear or wastage of capital assets—although, as the Majority state, such an allowance "has a connection with the year in which it falls due which is substantially less direct than that of the actual expenditure out of which a loss in the ordinary sense arises".[1] But as we have already pointed out, whenever expenditure of a *development* kind (i.e. expenditure not necessarily incurred in the production of those goods the sale proceeds of which constitute current receipts) is allowed as a deduction from current receipts in the calculation of taxable income the effect is that of a subsidy to the particular type of capital investment involved. In the case of initial and investment allowances, of expenditure on research and on improvements on agricultural land, the provision of such a subsidy—through allowances deductible from income tax—has been a matter of deliberate economic policy; in the case of the developmental expenses involved in advertising and entertaining the subsidy

[1] Para 503.

has come about as the incidental effect of the elastic definition of the Schedule D expenses rule. In any business the question whether a particular piece of developmental expenditure will result in a gain or a loss must, at the time when the investment is made, be regarded as a matter of speculation—albeit one over which the business itself has taken a sanguine view. The resultant gain or loss will emerge only in time. Yet at present capital investments, to the extent that they are subsidised, automatically appear as current losses in so far as expenditure upon them exceeds current receipts.

140. The difference between trading losses as at present defined, and capital losses for the purposes of a tax on capital gains, is seen particularly clearly if the case is considered of a man starting up a business in trade or farming. Such a man, if he intends to build up his business, will expect to invest capital in it, particularly in the early years. If his venture is successful he will in time be rewarded not only by a steady income from the total capital employed, but by an appreciation of the capital itself as the value of the business as a going concern is enhanced. Failure of the venture would be represented by a loss of capital as well as by an inadequate annual yield. A capital gains tax would take into account the capital gain or loss when it was realised. Under present arrangements, however, the more, and the more rapidly, a man is able to invest capital in building up his business, the larger are likely to be the "losses" which the revenue will share at the time the capital expenses are incurred; and the larger is likely to be the capital gain which will eventually ripen out of that capital expenditure, which the revenue will not share.

141. Thus it will be seen that even if capital gains were subjected to tax, the taxable capacity of those taxpayers who are able to deduct developmental expenditure from current receipts would still be under-assessed in relation to the taxable capacity of others. We do not think that this situation can be directly or completely remedied. Under a system of taxation of income which tends to discourage saving and risk-taking it has been found expedient in the general interest to encourage investment by the device of allowing developmental expenditure of various kinds to count as a deduction from taxable income. Furthermore, it must be recog-

nised that with existing accounting techniques it is not in all cases possible to draw a firm and satisfactory line between expenditures on income and on capital accounts, for purposes of determining net profits. This is particularly true of farming; but the problem is familiar also in connection with the distinction between maintenance and improvement of property (especially in the case of the owner-occupied house) and may in some degree be found wherever incomes are arrived at by deducting costs from receipts.

142. As already stated (paragraph 130) we believe that the earned income allowance, restricted to Schedule E and to those taxpayers assessed under Schedule D who opt for Schedule E treatment in regard to expenses, should be looked upon and used as rough compensation to those taxpayers who are at a relative disadvantage because of the generous treatment of expenses under Schedule D. In connection with the specific problem of losses we also hold the view that it is necessary in equity, and to prevent deliberate tax avoidance, to restrict the offset of losses to future income from the same source (as is largely the case at present with income assessed under Case VI of Schedule D), subject to an exception mentioned in paragraph 147 below.

143. Even if a trading loss were the result of an excess of current production costs (i.e., if there were no question of capital allowances or developmental expenditure entering the calculation of the loss) over current receipts, it would, in our view, be mistaken, both for reasons of equity and on economic grounds, to allow such a loss to be offset against other income. The effect of so doing must be to encourage the continuance of moribund or unproductive businesses at the expense of the revenue, and so ultimately of taxpayers in general. A business which is not moribund will be able to absorb its own losses, incurred in a bad trading year against the profits of future years. We agree with the Majority[1] that the ascertainment of business profits at fixed intervals of twelve months is an arbitrary process considering the continuous nature of business operations, so that to allow the carry-forward of losses— which means in effect that the taxpayer's account with the Revenue is a running account, and not one that is closed each year—"is an obvious concession to common sense".

[1] Para. 486.

144. When developmental expenditure enters into the calculation of a current trading "loss" the effect of allowing such a loss to be offset against income from other sources is that a taxpayer is able to build up a business at the direct expense of the revenue: in other words capital for the development of a man's business B is provided by the tax abatement on his income from source A. Part of a current tax bill is transformed into capital. Such an arrangement goes beyond the notion of subsidising certain types of investment to the extent of allowing expenditure upon them to be deducted from the receipts of the business concerned. In the latter case if the developmental expenditure exceeds net current receipts the business must find the whole of the capital out of which to make the excess expenditure. In the former case the excess expenditure may be largely paid for by the revenue. The situation in which a man is risking not his own capital, but part of his tax bill in respect of income from other sources, in investing in a business a sum greater than his current receipts from that business, appears to us to provide an incentive to take uneconomic risks together with wide opportunities for deliberate tax avoidance.

145. We believe that the method of allowing losses to be offset only against future income from the same source would substantially reduce such opportunities. Provisions that allow losses to be carried backwards against past income or offset against income from different sources in current or future years are all subject, in varying degrees, to the objection that they make it possible for the taxpayer to manipulate his affairs deliberately so as to minimise his tax liabilities. We are particularly opposed, on these grounds, to an extension of existing concessions to enable business losses to be offset against non-business income in future years. The Majority recommend[1] that unexhausted capital allowances or investment allowances should be permitted to be carried forward indefinitely as an offset against general income of future years. We believe that this suggestion is particularly open to the objection raised by the first Tucker Committee[2] that it opens the door to "avoidance devices, against which it would be difficult to devise a satisfactory antidote"; especially since, in the case of this particular proposal, the unexhausted capital allow-

[1] Para. 506.   [2] Cmd. 8189, para. 82.

D

ances do not even represent the actual current expenditure of a business, but merely allowances with respect to capital expenditure incurred in some past period. This recommendation would therefore offer new opportunities for reducing tax liabilities through the acquisition of unsuccessful or moribund concerns.

146. With regard to companies the recommendations of the first Tucker Report[1] implemented by Section 20 of the Finance Act of 1953, make it possible for the current profits and losses of a group of companies to be consolidated for tax purposes through the device of payments made by one company in a group to another. We are in agreement with these provisions but would like to propose that losses incurred by a subsidiary company should nevertheless be ignored in calculating the tax liability of the parent company in those cases where the acquisition of the subsidiary was made in the knowledge that it was incurring such a loss.

147. It is necessary to make an exception from the general rule that losses may only be offset against future income from the same source in those cases where a single business normally derives a surplus from one "source" at the cost of incurring a deficit in connection with activities that (technically) rank as a separate source, and where therefore the true commercial outcome of the business requires the aggregation of income from these separate sources. This may be the case with a bank whose trading expenses, in the form of interest paid to depositors, count as a separate source from that of its income from funds invested in securities, which is taxed by deduction at the source. For these reasons such concerns are already subject to special provisions[2] which enable them to set off taxed income of the current year against trading losses brought forward from previous years. We feel, however, that until capital gains in general are taxed on the lines we recommend the net losses arising out of security transactions of those financial concerns which are taxed on their capital gains as dealers in securities should not be allowed as an offset against taxed income, but only as a carry-forward against future income of the same kind.

[1] *Ibid.*, para. 294.
[2] Income Tax Act, 1952, s. 342 (4).

B. CAPITAL ALLOWANCES

148. As the Majority explain, the Royal Commission on the Income Tax of 1920 recommended that "no allowance should be granted to any asset other than an inherently wasting material asset which has been created by the expenditure of capital", and that no wastage should be recognised when the life of the wasting asset is estimated to be 35 years or longer.[1] The legislation introduced in 1944 and subsequent years has, however, extended the scope of these allowances much beyond the limits recommended by the 1920 Royal Commission, and the position has now been reached that, with a limited number of exceptions, an allowance is given for all material assets used in a business. As we stated earlier this creates an anomalous situation (a) partly because the allowances are only given in respect of material assets and not in respect of the wastage of capital expended in human education and training—a point which we have already discussed in paragraph 120 above; (b) because allowance is given for capital wastage, whilst no charge is imposed on capital gains.

149. With regard to the latter consideration the position would be fundamentally altered if our own proposals concerning the taxation of capital gains were adopted, and all gains realised on the sale of land and buildings brought into charge, as well as gains made on the sale of assets for which a capital allowance is now given. On condition that capital gains are brought into charge we feel that the principle put forward by the first Tucker Committee[2] that relief should be given "in respect of the wastage of all assets that are used up or consumed in the course of carrying on a business" can and should be given effect to. We are in agreement therefore with the Commission's recommendations concerning the depreciation allowance for commercial buildings, the introduction of a mining depletion allowance and an allowance for cutting and tunnelling work; and we also recommend a similar allowance with respect to the premiums paid for a lease.

150. As regards the mining depletion allowance and the allowance for premiums paid on leases, our recommendation is more directly dependent on the adoption of our proposals concerning the

[1] Cmd. 615, paras. 191, 186.   [2] Cmd. 8189, para. 193.

taxation of capital receipts in paragraph 71 above. We feel it would be wrong to allow the expense incurred in purchasing terminable rights as a capital outlay in a wasting asset unless the receipts from the sale of such rights are also made taxable. We do not dispute the Majority's contention[1] that under a system of progressive taxation the question whether a receipt should be treated as taxable or not, or whether an outlay should be treated as deductible or not, depends on its status in the hands of the taxpayer, and not on the question whether the payment itself receives symmetrical treatment in the hands of the other party to a particular transaction. Nevertheless we feel that if premiums on leases, or the capital sums spent on the acquisition of mineral rights, were to qualify as deductions from taxable income without the receipts being made taxable in the hands of the original owners of these rights, it would open the door to tax avoidance and tax evasion on the widest scale. The two parties to such transactions are not always at arm's length. A landowner, for example, on whose land minerals are discovered, could always form a company for their exploitation, and if the tax provisions are asymmetrical, he could reduce his aggregate net liability almost *ad libitum* by the simple expedient of charging his company as high a price as required for the acquisition of the rights of exploitation. The Majority believe that there would be no difficulty in making special provision for collusive sales.[2] But even in the case of genuine transactions, conducted at arm's length, the conversion of taxable income into tax-free capital receipts would be made a great deal easier than at present once the existing difference in the treatment, in the hands of the payer, as between annual payments and capital payments, is eliminated.

151. We fully concur with the recommendations of the Commission that, independently of the question of the general taxation of capital gains, the gains made on the sale of assets for which the tax system provides capital allowances should be charged to tax— i.e. the existing limitation on the balancing charge (imposed in connection with the sale of such assets) to the amount of the original cost should be withdrawn.[3] We do not oppose the special temporary concession recommended for the shipping industry.[4]

[1] Para. 34.   [2] Para. 440.   [3] Paras. 389–391.   [4] Para. 392.

We feel, however, that there is no reason why agricultural buildings and works, for which depreciation allowances are now given, should not be subject to a balancing charge in the same way as other assets, or why that charge should be limited to the original cost. We therefore recommend that the treatment of capital allowances given to agriculture should be assimilated to the treatment of capital allowances generally.

C. STOCK VALUATION

152. We are opposed to the recommendations of the Majority[1] that would permit trading stock to be valued for tax purposes by the lowest of three alternative methods of valuation, namely actual cost, market value, or value on the "base stock principle", provided only that the value of the closing stock of one accounting period as determined by the method adopted also serves as the opening figure for the next accounting period. The Majority also recommend that for the purpose of calculating the stock on the basis of "actual cost" the trader should have the option to choose from among four different methods for the ascertainment of actual cost (i.e. the actual cost of identifiable products where they are identifiable: the "first in, first out" method; a moving average cost; a standard or budgeted cost per unit; an estimated cost derived from the current selling price by deducting the normal profit margin from that price) "whichever is appropriate to the type of business and the nature of the stock concerned".[2]

153. Our objections to the Majority recommendations are based on grounds of equity (as between one trader and another, and as between traders and other taxpayers) as well as on grounds of economic expediency. Since the consideration of this problem involves rather complex issues it is necessary to set out the principles which in our view ought to govern the valuation of stock-in-trade for taxation purposes in some detail.

154. The governing consideration in ascertaining the trading profit of any particular year is to set against the receipts from the year's operations those costs which can be properly attributed to the goods the sales-proceeds of which formed those receipts. If

[1] In para. 473.　　[2] Appendix II, para. 2 (1).

the actual costs incurred in connection with each particular item sold could be separately identified these costs would form the sole permissible deduction from the receipts, and the valuation of trading stocks (at the opening or the closing date) would not be necessary for the purpose of ascertaining the year's profit. In a business with a continuing cycle of operations, this however will not normally be possible. The costs incurred over any given period will not correspond to the costs that can be properly attributed to the sales-proceeds of the period, since some part of the goods sold in any given year will have been acquired (and/or been in process of fabrication) in the previous year, whilst some part of the outlay incurred for materials, wages, etc., in the given year will be in respect of goods to be sold in the following year.

155. In these circumstances (which comprise of course the great majority of cases) the costs attributable to the goods sold in the given year can only be ascertained if the costs incurred in the year with respect to unsold goods are deducted from, and the costs incurred in the previous year with respect to goods sold in the present year are added to, the outlays actually incurred in the current year. There is only one reliable method for making such correction and that is to bring in the difference between the closing and opening stock as an addition to, or deduction from, the year's receipts (according as the difference is positive or negative), assuming that the items composing the stock at both dates are valued at actual cost.

156. The ascertainment of the actual cost of the items that compose the stock at the opening and at the closing date in turn can only be undertaken on the presumption that in a business with a continuing inflow of materials and labour and a continuing outflow of goods, the stocks of materials, goods in process and unsold finished goods in existence at any one time represent the unripened fruit of the most recent activities of the business. The fundamental reason why stocks need to be carried, and why the costs incurred in a year are not identifiable with the costs attributable to the goods sold in the year, is that production takes time. It follows from this that with the passage of time these various forms of stock are more or less continually depleted and continually replenished, so that the costs of the stocks extant at any point of

time are the costs ascertained by the "first in, first out" (F.I.F.O.) method of valuing stocks. Indeed no other assumption is consistent with the view that the activities of a concern consist of a recurrent cycle of operations and that production takes time.

157. We do not agree therefore with the Majority view that the assumption inherent in the "first in, first out" method—i.e. that the trader at any one time sells those things which have been longest in his hands—is an arbitrary one and "[does not derive] its validity from . . . the trader's physical operations".[1] The F.I.F.O. method of stock valuation is not just one of a number of alternative methods of valuing stock which may be appropriate to certain types of trade and certain types of stock, and not to others. Its justification lies in the basic view (which is not disputed) that stocks must be carried at the various stages of manufacturing and distribution precisely because the physical operations associated with those stages take time. We do not deny that occasionally traders (particularly wholesalers or retailers) sell their most recently acquired stock, and not the stock which has been longest on their shelves, but such cases are the incidental consequence of imperfect foresight, and not the peculiar properties of certain kinds of physical operations or of certain types of trading. Hence the only fair method of ascertaining the profit of different traders for tax purposes is by the use of an identical method of attribution of the costs which can be set against sales-proceeds, and this implies the general use of the F.I.F.O. method, not the use of differing methods according to the type of business or the nature of the stock carried. The only exception to this rule is to be found in those cases (like jewellers or antique dealers) where the actual cost incurred in connection with any particular item sold can be directly ascertained and the attribution of cost by means of calculations of stock changes is therefore unnecessary.

158. We should therefore like to support the suggestion put to the Commission by the Board of Inland Revenue that the valuation of stock by the so-called F.I.F.O. method should be made the general rule for valuing stocks in the ascertainment of trading profits for tax purposes. Departures from this rule ought only to be granted with the consent of the Revenue authorities and only

[1] Para. 452.

in those cases where a business cannot reasonably be expected to keep the records necessary for the ascertainment of stocks by the proper F.I.F.O. method. In actual fact the Revenue permits the use of simpler methods of stock valuation (on the basis of estimated cost or standard cost, etc.) in the case of small traders who have not the facilities for proper stock-keeping or book-keeping methods. But we feel it would lead to inequities if the choice of method with regard to the stock or any part of it were left to the option of the trader; and we deny the validity of reasoning according to which the "ideal" method of stock valuation varies according to the type of business. We cannot conceive of a case, for example, in which the nature of a trader's operations would make the ascertainment of stock value by reference to the current selling price with a deduction for the "normal profit margin" inherently more appropriate than the F.I.F.O. method.

159. The above paragraphs were confined to the question whether there should be any rule for ascertaining the value of stock in those cases where this value is presumed to reflect the actual cost of acquisition of that stock. But actual cost is not the only possible basis for valuing stock. As we mentioned earlier (paragraph 8 above), the Revenue authorities have for some time permitted the valuation of stocks on the basis of market value, when market value is below actual cost; and in addition, the Majority now recommend that traders should be free to adopt the "base-stock principle", which means valuing stock by the method described in paragraph 2 (4) of Appendix II to the Report.

160. As indicated earlier (paragraph 8 above) the valuation at market value when it is below actual cost is contrary to the general principle that only realised gains or losses are taken into account in calculating income for tax purposes. However, since stocks are normally turned over at reasonably short intervals, the permission to write down stocks in times of falling prices involves no more than the anticipation of a loss that would in any case be realised in the near future, normally in the following trading year. If, in the following year, prices rise again, the effect of writing down the stocks will be to attribute to that year a greater amount of profit than would have been attributable otherwise. We are satisfied therefore that the effect of this concession normally in-

volves no more than postponement of liability for a short period and we have no occasion to suggest a change in the existing practice in this respect.

161. When, however, we come to the Majority's major recommendation for the introduction of a variant of the so-called L.I.F.O. method of stock valuation we feel that strong arguments in equity as well as economic expediency argue against this proposal. The proposal amounts briefly to a permission to the trader to make a special stock provision each year representing the difference between the actual value of his stock and its base-cost value; the sum so set aside should be free of tax until it is subsequently drawn upon or until it is taxed in a manner analogous to the present balancing charge for fixed assets—either upon the cessation of the business, or upon a change in its character such that it no longer holds the kind of stock out of which the accumulated stock provision arose. The proposal thus amounts to exempting from taxation that element of profit which corresponds to the so-called "stock appreciation" as long as stocks of equivalent volume continue to be held and the business continues to exist.

162. The arguments for and against this proposal are rather different according as one supposes that the change in prices which gives rise to "stock appreciation" affects only a particular group of traders or whether it is part of a general change in the price level affecting all traders in more or less the same degree. In the former case any profit arising out of a rise in prices represents a genuine increase in the taxable capacity of the trader, both in relation to other traders and in relation to other taxpayers. For the mere fact that the cost of the stocks carried is higher at the closing date than it was at the opening date will not in itself involve an increase in the trading profit of the year in which the rise in prices occurred over and above the profit the trader would have realised if prices had not risen, unless he based his prices in the course of the year on the replacement cost, instead of the historical cost, of the articles sold. In that case, however, he must have made an abnormal margin of profit on some of his sales in the course of the year and there is no reason why he should not be taxed on it. On the other hand, if the trader sells on the basis of historical cost there will be no increase in his taxable profit for the

year, since the higher valuation of his closing stock (due to the rise
in prices) will be offset by a corresponding rise in his outlays during
the year relatively to his receipts. There seems to be no valid
reason why his profit for tax purposes should be reduced, as a
result of the rise in prices, below the figure which it would have
attained if prices had stayed the same. On either supposition
therefore the allowance for the difference in prices on the basis
of which stocks are valued reduces his taxable profit below his true
profit.

163. In the case of a general change in the level of prices (a
change in the value of money) it is arguable that the "true
profit" which is arrived at after replacing the physical stock of
capital used up in the course of production, is less than the
monetary profit based on a calculation of costs on a historical cost
basis. The arguments that may be advanced for exempting the
element of stock appreciation from taxation are identical in this
case with the arguments in favour of calculating depreciation of
fixed assets on the basis of replacement costs. The Commission
rejected the proposals for the replacement cost basis of calculating
depreciation for reasons that we need not repeat here and which
seem to us to be decisive.[1] In our view it follows inescapably that
the claim to exempt the element of stock appreciation from taxation on grounds of inflation ought equally to be rejected.

164. The Majority recommendation does not formally concede
that claim, since the profits that are relieved from tax under their
scheme do not escape taxation altogether: they are placed in a
suspense account, so to speak, which is to be drawn on as and when
prices fall, the volume of stocks carried is reduced, or the
business is liquidated. However, in contrast to the L.I.F.O. system
operating in the United States (where a trader who has once
chosen this system cannot subsequently resort to an actual cost or
market value basis should that prove to be to his advantage), the
balance in this "suspense account" can never become negative:
although a trader would be taxed less than at present in times of
rising prices he could not incur a higher cumulative tax liability
if prices fell. The option, therefore, while it may or may not
benefit the taxpayer, could never benefit the revenue. Since

[1] See particularly paras. 355–356 as well as paras. 341–342 of the Report.

modern business corporations have a continuing life; since the real volume of production can be expected to be rising over time; since the long-run trend of prices is more likely to be rising than falling, the expectation is that the adoption of this recommendation would mean both a permanent loss and a growing loss of revenue over time.

165. In the six years 1948–53, according to official estimates,[1] the element of stock appreciation in the rise in the value of stocks (excluding stocks held by the central government) amounted to £m1,640, or an average of £m273 a year. Assuming that the scheme now recommended by the Majority had been in force in those years and that corporations and individual traders would have taken full advantage of the facilities offered by the scheme, there would have been an annual loss of revenue of something of the order of £150 millions a year. If this loss of revenue had been made good by a general increase in the level of taxation it would have involved a redistribution of the burden of taxation from traders to the rest of the community. If it had been made good by a specific increase of taxation on those groups who mainly benefited from the scheme (by an increase in the rates of the profits tax, for example) it would have meant that the disincentive effects of high marginal rates of taxation would have operated more sharply, with little, if any, compensating gain in more equitable distribution of the tax burden as between different traders. It can be argued of course that prices will not increase in the future at the same rate as they did over the past six years or that they may not increase at all. In that case the adoption of this scheme would neither cause a loss of revenue nor be of any benefit to the traders concerned.

166. There is finally, the consideration advanced by Miss Sutherland and Professor Hicks that the adoption of the scheme would be contrary to the national interest. As they say in their Reservation—"the right course is to keep businesses short of funds during the time of pressure, and to let them off more easily later; this is what F.I.F.O. does, while L.I.F.O. works in the other, the wrong, direction". We fully associate ourselves with this point of view.

[1] *National Income and Expenditure*, 1946–53, Table 48.

D. DOUBLE TAXATION RELIEF

167. The principle underlying double taxation relief raises complicated issues both from the point of view of equity and from the point of view of the economic consequences of the tax provisions. We do not share the view that it is inherently inequitable that the profit earned in one country by the resident of another country should be subjected to tax both by the country where the profits originate and by the country where the owner resides. The right of any sovereign authority to impose taxes on income arising in its territory cannot be disputed. Such taxes are causally indistinguishable from the numerous other factors—such as the level of local wages—which affect the profitability of foreign investment. If foreign taxes are treated as deductible expenses in arriving at the taxable income of an individual for purposes of home taxation, the income received by the individual from various sources, home and foreign, is treated in the same way—which is as it should be. For under a system of progressive taxation, as the Majority explain in another context,[1] "income tax is nothing but the sum of all the taxes on each individual, each computed separately according to the total income and personal circumstances of that individual". Hence the question whether any particular streamlet of money has or has not been taxed on its way to the owner by a different taxing authority is no more relevant for deciding what his total tax liability should be for the purposes of home taxation than any of the numerous other factors that affect the amount of income received from particular sources.

168. The justification for double taxation relief—which treats the foreign taxes not as expenses in arriving at the taxable profit, but as tax credits deductible in full from the taxes payable at home—lies not in the realm of equity, but in the encouragement it affords to the flow of international investment. Since the encouragement of international investment for the purpose of developing the backward areas of the world is a prime objective of our national policy; and since the principle of double taxation relief has now been firmly established through numerous international agreements, we do not suggest that it would be either

[1] Para. 33.

practicable or desirable to go back on the whole principle in the foreseeable future even though the relief causes a loss of revenue of the order of £m100 a year. Nevertheless we feel that some of the peculiarly anomalous features of the system as it has developed since before the war could and should be abolished. While the need for an ample flow of international investment may justify the abolition of "double taxation"—that is to say, the removal of the *discouragement* to foreign investment—we do not see the justification for arrangements which secure privileged treatment for foreign investment as compared with home investment, or which have the effect of granting relief to a British resident from such foreign taxes as would not be offset against his personal tax liability under the laws of the foreign country where the taxes are imposed.

169. Thus we regard it as anomalous that a British shareholder of an American company (even though he be a minority shareholder) should be able to claim as an offset against his British income tax and surtax liability, not only the American "withholding tax" (i.e., the tax deducted from the dividend at source, which is analogous to the standard rate of income tax deducted from dividends in this country) but his aliquot share of the United States corporation profits tax, which under the laws of the United States is not credited (except to a nominal extent) against the personal tax liability of an American shareholder. As a result of this arrangement a United Kingdom shareholder of an American company enjoys a higher effective dividend on American shares than the American shareholder. Since the prices of American securities are determined in the American and not the British stock markets, the arrangement is not only inequitable but provides an unhealthy incentive for British investors to invest in American companies since the yield of American shares is made artificially attractive relatively to British shares, owing to these peculiar tax provisions. It is true that the objections on economic grounds to such arrangements are mitigated, though not removed, when they depend, as at present, upon reciprocal agreement. Under existing arrangements the United States shareholder in British companies is equally entitled to credit his aliquot share of the United Kingdom profits tax against his United States income tax liability, although no such facility is offered to the British

shareholder of such companies. Such reciprocity, however, in no way affects the inequities resulting from such arrangements amongst resident taxpayers in either country.

170. The Majority recognise that "there is nothing inherently inadmissible in the idea of taxing a dividend as a source of personal income altogether distinct from the profits from which it is derived and without regard to the tax imposed on those profits in the hands of the company". They also take the view that the argument in favour of extending such concessions without regard to reciprocity "does not appear . . . to be specially compelling".[1] Nevertheless they recommend that "the indirect tax behind a minority shareholder's dividend should be generally recognised as ranking in principle for unilateral relief".[2] Our own recommendation is that the existing arrangements—under which such indirect taxes qualify for relief from personal taxation as a result of bilateral agreements or of the special provisions relating to Commonwealth territory—far from being extended without regard to reciprocity, should be brought to an end. We feel that no taxes should be credited against personal income tax liability in the United Kingdom which are not so credited in the country where the profits originate and the "indirect" taxes are imposed.

171. We are equally opposed to the Majority's suggestion[3] that taxes imposed by a state, province, canton, or other subdivision of a territory or even municipal income or profits taxes, should qualify for relief quite irrespective of whether or not such local income taxes are credited against the taxes of the central Government. We feel that there is no justification for granting relief from local taxes in those cases where the Government of the foreign country does not recognise the right to such relief in regard to its own income taxes; and there is no case for giving specific relief in those cases where it does, since then the relief for such taxes is already afforded in connection with the taxes imposed by the central Government. It does not seem to us material whether a particular foreign country imposes local government taxes in the form of special taxes on property (as in this country) or in the form of taxes on income and profits. If such local government taxes are not credited against income tax liability

[1] Para. 707.   [2] Para. 708.   Para. 701.

in the case of home income, we do not see that they should be so credited with respect to foreign income.

172. We believe that if our recommendations concerning company taxation (in Section III above) were accepted it would be possible to adopt simpler and more rational rules concerning the relief from foreign taxation. We recommend, as the principle to be followed, that the relief given to individuals should be limited to the taxes imposed on individuals and the relief given to companies should be limited to the corresponding taxes imposed on companies. This means that companies would be entitled to relief on the whole of the taxes imposed on their foreign branches where the profits of those branches are subjected to United Kingdom taxation; while in the case of non-resident subsidiaries which are not subjected to United Kingdom taxation the relief would be limited to those taxes which are attributable to the dividends received from the foreign subsidiaries. The foreign tax relief credited to individuals on the other hand should be limited to such taxes (as, for example, the so-called "withholding taxes" imposed on dividends) as are intended by the foreign Government to rank as direct taxes imposed on individuals, and which would, therefore, be credited against the individual tax liability of the shareholder if he were a resident of that country.

173. Our recommendations concerning company taxation would also remove the anomaly, to which reference was made earlier, as a result of which the benefit of double tax relief is only available in full to shareholders whose total tax liability is equal to or exceeds the amount deducted at source. If relief from foreign taxation were given to companies against their corporation profits tax liability, and the United Kingdom corporation profits tax were not itself credited against the income tax liability of individuals, small and large shareholders and tax-exempt shareholders (like charities or pension funds) would benefit alike from double taxation relief. The anomalies resulting from the existing arrangements, particularly in the case of a preference shareholder who is exempt from tax, are outlined by the Majority in paragraphs 715–718 of the Report. The Majority conclude that the "stubborn fact is that a preference shareholding in a company enjoying the benefit of double taxation relief is not, because of the

tax consequences, a suitable investment for an exempt person and we are bound to say that the real remedy for the situation complained of is a change of investment".[1] Preference shares, however, may be a peculiarly suitable form of investment for institutions like charities or pension funds; and we do not feel that the problem is adequately met by the suggestion that such bodies should refrain from investing their funds in companies which enjoy substantial double taxation relief. This inevitably has the effect of narrowing the field of suitable investments for the funds of such institutions. However, this problem would disappear altogether if the present artificial link between company taxation and personal taxation were removed.

£. OVERSEAS PROFITS

174. The arguments against the exemption of overseas profits from taxation, on both equity considerations and economic grounds are set out in paragraphs 646–655 and paragraph 664 of the Report. These parts of the Report were drawn up with our participation and we have no wish to enlarge upon the views expressed there. We feel it necessary, however, to state our view that the particular recommendation adopted by the Majority cannot, with any certainty, be described as a less comprehensive measure than other alternatives considered, in so far as the definition of "overseas trade corporations" is left vague at precisely those points where exact definition is required to determine the scope of the proposed concession. The scheme which commends itself to the Majority is "one that would give exemption to the profits of special 'overseas trade corporations' on the lines that we have discussed in paragraphs 673 to 677 above";[2] and one in which "only such activities within the United Kingdom should be within the exemption as the economic interests of the country are seen to demand".[3]

175. Our view might be different if the conception of an "overseas trade corporation" were intended to be, and could effectively be, confined to the cases categorised in paragraph 674 of the Report. We appreciate the economic advantage of removing a

[1] Para. 718.　　　[2] Para. 689.　　　[3] Para. 690 (2).

discouragement to maintaining the central management of a concern in this country in the case of a British company that derives all, or substantially all, its income from overseas operations—as for example in the case of a British concern operating local public utilities in foreign countries—which may desire to transfer surplus funds to this country for the purchase of supplies and equipment, or for temporary investment.

176. But as the Majority point out[1] once "overseas trade corporations" are defined so as to include "those concerns which extract or produce commodities overseas but bring them to this country for sale or the export industries which manufacture here but sell abroad", limitation of the concession depends upon formulating and administering fine distinctions. In the case of an importing business the distinctions must be drawn between trading *with* and trading *in* this country—distinctions "themselves dependent upon the terms of business with brokers, commission agents, etc." In the case of exporting businesses the problems of definition and administration are even more formidable and the consequences of inadequacies in these respects far more serious. The section of "overseas trading corporations" which represents "merely the exporting side of the United Kingdom manufacturer who sells some of his goods abroad"[2] must be so circumscribed as to exclude any company, or subsidiary, which contracts foreign sales in this country. Otherwise it would be open to any United Kingdom manufacturing or wholesaling business to conduct its foreign sales through a special subsidiary: with the result that the concession, far from being less comprehensive than alternative proposals, would tend to exempt from taxation the profits earned on exports generally. It is difficult to see how a distinction between selling merchandise to overseas customers and "sending it overseas for sale there" could be made, or operated, without reintroducing the condition that the corporation in question must maintain a permanent overseas establishment—with all the attendant difficulties and disadvantages, including the provision of a tax incentive to set up such establishments abroad, described to the Commission in detail by the Board of Inland Revenue and referred to in paragraphs 668

[1] Paras. 675 and 676.   [2] Para. 676.

and 669 of the Report. In any case, as the Majority state[1] this part of the scheme "revives again the administrative difficulties of ascertaining satisfactorily what are the real profits of a branch that purchases goods from its head office at a price and under conditions that do not represent open trading".

177. We believe that adoption of this recommendation would expose the Government of the United Kingdom to the accusation that, contrary to international commitments, it subsidises its exports through preferential tax measures. It would be the more difficult for the Government to refute such an accusation since it would be impossible to ensure that the price at which the merchandising subsidiary obtained goods from the manufacturer covered both the cost and the profit properly attributable to the manufacturing activities of the concern.

178. It is not of course possible to make any close estimate of the cost of the proposed concession since its scope remains indefinite; but it is possible to form an idea of its order of magnitude. The Board of Inland Revenue estimate the taxes now payable by United Kingdom resident companies on profits earned overseas (excluding shipping and insurance firms) at "somewhat higher than" £m65. Some part of this loss (which the Board put at £m20) would be recoverable when the profits came to be distributed to United Kingdom shareholders in the form of dividends, although the task of separating dividends paid out of such profits would not be an easy one where the dividends reach the individual shareholders through parent companies who would not, as such, be exempted from tax. On the other hand as the dividends of non-resident subsidiaries to resident parent companies would no longer be taxable (since the controlling shares of such subsidiaries could be held by holding companies that fell within the scope of overseas trade corporations) there would be a further loss which the Board estimate at £m10. According to the precise definition of "overseas trading corporations" something less or something more than the resultant estimate of £m55 would be lost to the revenue. It is not possible to say whether any further allowance should be made to cover insurance firms and an extra cost resulting from the reorganisa-

1 *Ibid.*

tion of United Kingdom concerns (particularly export businesses) to take advantage of the concession; nor whether, in the event, the cost would tend to be inflated by the transference of some proportion of profits properly attributable to manufacturing operations at home to merchandising subsidiaries falling within the scope of the proposed concession.

179. We agree with the view that the variety of practice of the tax treatment of the so-called "overseas profits" in different countries, described by the Majority, along with the growing practice of export subsidisation in its manifold forms, puts this country at a disadvantage in its overseas trading activities. We believe, however, that the remedy should be sought in international efforts to secure the suppression of such practices, and the adoption of conventions ensuring uniformity of treatment, rather than in their imitation.

VI. OTHER ISSUES CONCERNING THE TAXATION OF INCOMES

A. EXPENSE ALLOWANCES AND BENEFITS IN KIND

180. While an employee assessed under Schedule E can only claim expenses that qualify under the rigid rule as necessary expenses incurred in the performance of duties, it is open to any employer to pay an allowance for expenses incurred by the employee on his behalf. From the point of view of the employer such payments are outlays incurred for the purpose of trade and are chargeable against his profits in much the same way as any other kind of business outlay. From the point of view of the employee, until the special legislation of 1948 was introduced, such an allowance was not a taxable receipt even if it was given for the purpose of outlays that would not have been deductible had the employee paid for them out of his own salary. In theory if the money so obtained was not laid out for business purposes at all, but was merely a disguised form of remuneration, it was open to the Revenue to challenge the return made by the em-

ployee and to claim that the expense allowance received was part of his salary; but since such allowances were not included in a taxpayer's return of income, the Revenue would frequently have no knowledge of such payments at all. Even if they had, as the Majority explain,[1] it would have been very difficult for the Revenue to challenge any but the most obvious cases, or to make good their challenge before the appeal Commissioners.

181. In our view the form in which a person obtains a receipt—whether it is called a wage or salary, or an expense allowance—ought not to make any difference to the question of whether the receipt is taxable or not. Equally the extent to which a taxpayer is able to claim expenses against his receipts should be the same, irrespective of whether these expenses are met out of his regular salary or out of a special allowance provided by the employer for the purpose. If different rules apply to the deductibility of expenses according to whether the employer makes provision for those expenses in fixing the basic salary of the employee, or whether he makes a special provision in the form of supplementary payments, avenues are opened for tax avoidance through the masquerading of remuneration as expense allowances.

182. The 1948 legislation was intended to eliminate such differences of treatment by providing that all allowances received by certain classes of taxpayers should be added to their taxable incomes, and deductions could be claimed for expenses actually incurred, in so far as those expenses satisfied the general rule of expenses applicable to Schedule E. The provisions of this legislation were limited, however, to directors of companies and to employees with emoluments (including the expense allowance received) of over £2,000 a year. We understand that this limitation did not rest on any principle but on administrative considerations. It was thought that the circumstances, in which the opportunity and temptation occurred to pay or receive remuneration under the guise of an expense allowance, were broadly limited to those in which members of the boards of companies were in a position to determine the form of their own remuneration; or those in which companies might seek to attract and recruit high salary earners by the offer of tax-free expense

[1] In para. 226.

allowances. We understand it to be the view of the Revenue authorities that these two classes do, in fact, cover most of the likely recipients of regular expense allowances.

183. The 1948 Act also empowered the Revenue to give dispensations from the provisions of the Act in cases where a company satisfies the Tax Inspector that the payments made to an employee are of a character that would not attract additional tax liability if the provisions of the Act were fully applied. Such dispensations can, however, at any time be revoked. We understand that, in the period following the initial introduction of this legislation, dispensations were rather freely given as a matter of administrative necessity, but as the administrative pressure on the tax offices has gradually eased, a number of such dispensations have been withdrawn. We gather that such dispensations have not been given, and are not being given, in the case of entertainment allowances or for foreign travel.

184. We do not agree with the view of the Majority[1] that "it is right that Inspectors should be encouraged to make use of their powers [to grant such dispensations] even with regard to classes of payment that are at present altogether excluded from dispensation". We believe, on the contrary, that equity requires that the provisions of the 1948 Act should be rigorously applied; and that consequently the dispensations granted under the Act should be confined to limited classes of payments in which the likelihood of the payments not qualifying as deductible expenses under Schedule E rule is negligible.

185. We dissent from the recommendation of the Majority[2] according to which directors receiving less than £2,000 a year and owning or controlling less than 5 per cent. of the ordinary share capital of a director-controlled company should be exempted from the provisions of the 1948 legislation. We do not share their view either that the legislation is "discriminatory" or that its incidence is "conspicuously unfair to the part-time director".[3] For the really important consequence of the 1948 legislation is not in the field of benefits in kind, but in the obligation to include receipts in the form of expense allowances along with salaries and other forms of remuneration in the taxpayer's return of income.

[1] Para. 235.   [2] Paras. 218, 228.   [3] Para. 217.

Looked at from this point of view, the 1948 legislation could only be regarded as discriminatory or unfair in so far as there are important groups of persons who are in receipt of such allowances but to whom the provisions of the 1948 Act do not at present apply. We understand that this is not the case, and that the Act does in fact embrace most persons to whom such allowances are likely to be paid. If however this were not so, the remedy should be sought in extending the scope of the legislation to cases which are not covered at present, and not in restricting its scope in a manner that is bound to increase the inequity of the tax system.

186. In our view part-time directors represent a class of taxpayer particularly liable, in the absence of special restrictions, to receive part of their remuneration in the form of tax-free expense allowances. The restriction of the exemption proposed by the Majority to directors receiving less than £2,000 a year raises a special problem in its application to part-time directors, since many such directors hold multiple directorships and may, therefore, have an income much in excess of £2,000 a year even though their emoluments from any single directorship are below that amount. The Board estimate the cost of removing non-controlling directors with emoluments of less than £2,000 from the provision of the Act as likely to be less than £m2 a year. Though £m2 may not be a very large sum in relation to other reforms proposed, we feel bound to point out that it is a loss of revenue that arises not from any change in the concept of taxable income but from a decision to relax the rules under which the tax laws are administered.

187. Equally we are unable to follow the Majority in their view that the attempt of the Revenue authorities to limit allowable expenses to the additional expenditure incurred as a result of business travelling or entertainment should be abandoned since there are no means by which the hypothetical savings of a person can be satisfactorily determined in such cases. As the Majority put it, "Rule 9 assumes that expenses are represented by actual expenditure, not by a computation which offsets expenditure hypothetically saved".[1] This is true but it ought also to be borne in mind that the literal application of Rule 9 (i.e., the Schedule

[1] Para. 231.

E expenses rule) would exclude the deduction of any particular item of expenditure that was not "wholly" and "exclusively" incurred for business purposes. We understand that the Revenue authorities, as a normal practice, allow the apportionment of particular items of expense which were only partly incurred for business purposes between a deductible business-part and a non-deductible non-business-part of such expenditure; and if such apportionment is permitted as a matter of administrative concession, it logically follows that deductible expenses should be confined to the additional expenditure incurred by a person in the performance of his duties. No doubt there are cases in which the so-called "home saving" is negligible, but there are other cases in which it may be far from negligible, and we do not feel that it would be equitable if the attempt to confine allowances to the additional expenditure incurred by the taxpayer were generally abandoned.

188. We agree with the Majority's recommendation[1] that the present exemption granted to the directors, etc., of charitable bodies or non-trading concerns from the operation of the 1948 Act should be removed, though we are doubtful about the suggestion that the special exemption granted to employees of educational establishments or local authorities should equally be removed. We have in mind the case of the schoolmaster or Headmaster who has received benefits in kind from time immemorial, and for reasons entirely unconnected with motives of tax avoidance. We feel that there is not sufficient justification for the disturbance that would be caused to the finances of educational institutions if these benefits were brought into charge, unless it were part of a wider reform which brought benefits in kind generally within the tax net.

189. We should like to recommend that the Board of Inland Revenue should publish annually in their Report figures relating to the operation of the 1948 legislation, showing (i) the number of cases in which assessments have been raised as a result of the operation of the Act; (ii) the total amount of expenses claimed in these cases; (iii) the amount of such expenses that were disallowed.

190. With regard to benefits in kind, we are in agreement with

[1] Paras. 221, 228.

the Majority's view[1] that the "provision of untaxable benefits in kind is capable of becoming an abuse of the tax system". We are also in agreement with their view[2] that it is "probable that a changeover to a system that assessed and taxed all benefits in kind would involve a considerable disturbance of the wage structure, with ultimate adjustments that might leave the relative rewards much as before". In the circumstances we agree that the tendency to provide benefits in kind on a more extensive scale needs careful watching; and that developments that may be regarded primarily as forms of tax avoidance might have to be controlled by disallowing the related expenditure in the employer's profit assessment. In our view one such development that has already aroused widespread public comment is the growing use by employees and their families of motor cars provided by the employer.

B. SUPERANNUATION TAX RELIEF

Extension of Superannuation Tax Relief

191. The Majority consider that the main justification for superannuation tax relief lies in the fact that the man whose income is derived from his personal earnings must in effect regard some provision for his retirement and the care of his dependants as a charge upon those earnings.[3] They accordingly endorse the majority recommendations of the second Tucker Committee that analogous tax relief should be extended to all those classes of earners who are at present denied it: self-employed persons, controlling and other directors, and employees having inadequate pension rights or none at all. These recommendations commend themselves to the Majority as required for the sake of an equitable distribution of the tax burden between different taxpayers; and they do not think the case for them is displaced by what is said in the reservation made by the minority of the Tucker Committee.[4]

192. It does not seem to us, however, that equity is attained by making superannuation tax reliefs available to so wide a range of taxpayers without regard to the circumstances of the recipients. These reliefs already represent a substantial tax concession

---

[1] Para. 222.   [2] Para. 215.   [3] Para. 70.   [4] Para. 75.

involving an annual sacrifice of revenue of the order of £m100; and according to the estimate made by the Inland Revenue for the Tucker Committee[1] the extension of these reliefs to cover the classes of persons not at present covered would, on reasonable assumptions, cost a further £m55–£m70. Tax reliefs of this magnitude should not be recommended unless it is clear that the circumstances of the persons to whom the reliefs are to be extended are broadly comparable from the standpoint of superannuation with those of the persons already covered. In at least two classes of the persons concerned—the self-employed and controlling directors—we do not think this is the case. The circumstances we have particularly in mind refer to the age of retirement and the possession of capital assets.

193. Unlike the general run of employees for whom the retiring ages are determined in advance by the employer, self-employed persons and controlling directors are not subject to a conventional retiring age. The 1948 Companies Act requires[2] that a director shall normally retire at 70, but it may be little more than a formality in the case of a controlling director to obtain the consent of a general meeting of the company to his continuance in office. Moreover, as pointed out by the Tucker Committee,[3] retirement in these cases may be only a matter of degree. The individual proprietor of a business or a controlling director of a company may reasonably expect the business or company to go on supporting him until his death; or he may arrange late in life to attend only part-time at the business and yet go on drawing an income or salary from it.

194. In the second place self-employed persons and controlling directors are in the majority of cases necessarily possessed of capital assets which can be realised on retirement to provide funds for support in old age. Those assets will usually be in the form of buildings, machinery, stock and goodwill, or in the case of controlling directors they will take the form of shares representing those assets. In the course of a working life and during periods of rising prices, as we argued earlier (paragraph 42), these may exhibit considerable capital appreciation. It is true that many self-employed persons will be in a small way of business and the

---

[1] Cmd. 9063, paras. 449, 469.   [2] Section 185.   [3] Cmd. 9063, para. 314.

value of their physical assets and goodwill will not be large; but it is the value of their capital assets relatively to the standard of living they expect in retirement that is important, not the absolute value.

195. Moreover, the possession of capital assets assumes greater significance when superannuation tax reliefs are made available because under the existing system no effort is made to ensure that the savings in the form of superannuation contributions represent genuine savings. The Majority recognise the need to avoid giving relief "for what is really delusive saving",[1] and we agree with them that in respect of existing superannuation reliefs it can be presumed that superannuation contributions will normally represent a true saving of income.[2] However, if superannuation relief were extended to cover self-employed persons and controlling directors there is a greater risk that the additional tax concessions would be taken advantage of to substitute tax-free savings for other forms of savings.

196. We would admit one qualification to the above arguments in respect of those self-employed persons, deriving their remuneration from a profession or vocation, who are taxed under Case II of Schedule D. Professional remuneration is in general dependent upon personal qualifications and involves little or no capital. Although the general absence of an enforceable retirement age remains as an important differentiating factor, we think there is a case for extending superannuation tax relief to these persons. It was noted in the reservation to the Tucker Committee's Report[3] that a number of professional Associations have expressed themselves as willing and able to organise and administer superannuation funds on analogous lines to those set up under Section 32, Finance Act, 1921.[4] We agree with the view expressed there that such funds should be admitted if it is found practicable to frame and carry out arrangements acceptable to the Board of Inland Revenue.

197. With this qualification, we are strongly opposed to the recommendations of the second Tucker Committee for extending superannuation tax relief to self-employed persons and controlling directors.

[1] Para. 67.   [2] Para. 66.   [3] Cmd. 9063, pp. 152–153.
[4] See now Income Tax Act, 1952, s. 379.

Lump-sum Benefits on Retirement

198. We also disagree with the views of the Majority on the Tucker Committee's recommendation that it should be permissible for an approved superannuation scheme to pay, in a tax-free lump sum, up to a quarter of the total benefit due on retirement, subject to a maximum of £10,000.[1] The Majority agree with the Tucker Committee that such tax-free payments are anomalous and feel that they cannot approve the making of schemes that allow a substantial part of superannuation relief to be capitalised in tax-free form. At the same time they consider that expectations have been raised by existing practice and that a complete reversal of the practice cannot be achieved at short notice or without some provision for cases of hardship. The solution that they favour, therefore, is that the £10,000 maximum proposed should apply to members of schemes existing at the date when the new regulations are introduced, but that a much smaller maximum, say £2,000, ought to be applied to all future entrants.[2]

199. We do not believe that there is anything to be said either on grounds of logic or of equity in favour of a figure of £2,000 rather than one of £10,000. The only satisfactory way of dealing with a concession that is admitted to be anomalous is to abolish it altogether. We accordingly recommend that it should be made a condition of approval of a superannuation scheme by the Inland Revenue that it should afford only pension benefits to future entrants; and that statutory superannuation schemes should be amended to ensure that all future entrants receive their benefits in pension form. Existing members of superannuation schemes with contractual rights to lump-sum benefits on retirement would not be affected by this recommendation.

Compensation for Loss of Office and Ex Gratia Payments

200. We agree with the Majority that it would not make sense to have one scheme for taxing sums paid by way of compensation for loss of office, and another scheme for taxing ex gratia lump sums given to employees on termination of service. We also agree with them that these payments should be treated as taxable income, but not as income of the year when they are received.

[1] Cmd. 9063, paras. 160–162.   [2] Para. 73.

On the other hand, we cannot agree with their recommendation that, as a concession, one-quarter of these lump-sum benefits up to £2,000 should be tax-free. There is no more reason for allowing part of these sums to be tax-free than there is for allowing tax-free lump sums in the case of contractual retirement benefits.

201. We accordingly recommend that the whole of the payments by way of compensation for loss of office as defined in paragraph 244 of the Report, and ex gratia lump-sum benefits of the kind dealt with in paragraph 252 of the second Tucker Committee's Report[1] should be charged to tax (by top-slicing by reference to a period of five years).

C. ALIENATION OF INCOME BY MEANS OF COVENANTS

202. The British system of taxation is almost unique in recognising a payment voluntarily undertaken by the taxpayer as a charge on his income, provided that payment (i) is made under a promise backed by a deed of covenant extending to a period of more than six years; (ii) is not made in favour of an unmarried infant of the covenantor; (iii) is not in exchange for value received from (or goods or services rendered by) the recipient. The intention of the law is thus to treat voluntary gifts and contributions, provided they are intended to be continued for longer periods, as charges and not as applications of the income of the taxpayer.

203. As the Majority point out,[2] the distinction between a charge on income which is treated as a reduction of income, and an application of income which is not, is a fine one. Gifts are of benefit to the giver, as well as the receiver; and the whole distinction between gifts and compensation introduces serious administrative difficulties. So long as income tax was a flat-rate tax, and tax was in any case deducted at source, nothing much depended on the manner of treatment of such gifts. But with the introduction of super-tax in 1909–10, the justification of the prevailing legal conception could rightly be called into question as a matter of principle, quite apart from the fact that it invites the dressing up of real exchanges in the guise of one-sided transfers.

204. Since 1922 a number of restrictions has been introduced

[1] Cmd. 9063.   [2] Para. 144.

circumscribing the conditions under which the transfer of income by means of covenants is valid for tax purposes, the general intent of which is to counter tax avoidance in cases where the payments made under covenants merely relieve the covenantor of his own expenditure. Since 1946 covenants made in favour of charities or of agents and employees of the taxpayer are no longer recognised for surtax purposes though they are still recognised for income tax. As the Majority point out[1] it is not easy to see on what ground of principle a transfer of income should be disallowed to charities and corporate bodies while a similar transfer of incomes to individuals is allowed.

205. We do not agree with the Majority's conclusion[2] that covenants "play a useful part" in the tax system. At the same time we recognise that they have become so extensively used in our tax system that their sudden abolition might cause financial hardship in the case of many families, whose standard of expenditure has become adapted to the effective reduction in their tax bill secured by means of covenants.

206. It is possible to argue also that so long as no obstacles are placed in the way of transfers of property *inter vivos* the denial of any recognition to transfers of income places the man whose income comes from work and not from property in a relatively unfavourable position. This argument does not justify, however, the recognition of covenants in the case of unearned incomes. When a gift or contribution is made by a man of property it is impossible to say whether this gift or contribution was met out of income or out of capital; yet the system of covenants makes it possible to claim a rebate of tax on the former even though it was a charge on the latter.

207. Though the matter of property transfers is outside the Commission's terms of reference and we do not therefore wish to make any recommendations in regard to it, we should like to record our view that the unhindered freedom accorded under our system to an individual to divest himself of property by means of *inter vivos* gifts (subject only to stamp duty in the case of documentary transfers) is hardly in congruity with the heavy taxation on property passing by inheritance. The remedy here is therefore

[1] Para. 148 (3). [2] Para. 150.

to supplement the existing Death Duties with a gift tax on *inter vivos* transfers, as is done in the United States. If this were done, any justification for the retention of the system of income transfers by means of covenants would disappear. (Under the laws of the United States, it is not possible at all for a taxpayer to assign his income to someone else for tax purposes except in the case of alimony or separation allowances paid by husbands to wives.)

208. We believe therefore that our present system of inheritance taxes needs reviewing in connection with the question of income and property transfers generally; and the question of the tax treatment of voluntary transfers of income by means of covenants could only be satisfactorily explored in connection with such a wider inquiry.

209. As an interim measure we should like to endorse the recommendations of the Majority to the effect that (i) covenants made out in favour of discretionary trusts should no longer be recognised for tax purposes;[1] and (ii) that formal annual declarations should be required by both covenantor and covenantee, in the case of covenants made out in favour of family members of the covenantor, to the effect that there exists no agreement or understanding, whether or not regarded as having legal force, by virtue of which the benefit of any part of the payments is returned, directly or indirectly, to the covenantor or any other person designated by him.[2] We would like to recommend that this obligation should extend to covenants made out in favour of any relative of the covenantor, and that the declaration should take the form of a statutory declaration upon oath.

210. We should also like to recommend that the amount of covenanted income the transfer of which is recognised for the purpose of the surtax assessment of the covenantor should be limited to £500 a year in the case of any one beneficiary. We believe that a limitation of this kind would be fully justified, and would represent a logical extension of the provisions already in force in the case of covenants in favour of charities.

---

[1] Para. 157.   [2] Para. 161.

D. CHARITIES

211. We entirely agree with the Majority of the Commission that to introduce into the tax code a definition of a charity "at once more limited and precise" than the present definition is a necessary and practicable reform. We also wish to associate ourselves with the Reservation on the subject by Mr. Gates and Professor Hicks recommending that the tax exemption of the income of charities should not be complete regardless of the level of the standard rate of tax, but "that charities should receive total exemption from tax only up to a fixed rate, say, 5s. od. in the £; after which they should pay tax at a rate equal to one-half of the amount by which the standard rate of income tax exceeds 5s. od."

E. SCHEDULE A CHARGE ON DWELLING-HOUSES

212. Apart from the question of premiums on leases referred to in paragraph 150 above, we are in agreement with the Commission's recommendations concerning Schedules A and B, except on one point: the charge to be imposed on the owner-occupier of a dwelling-house. The Majority recommend, in accordance with the suggestion made to the Commission by the Board of Inland Revenue, that the Schedule A charge on the owner-occupier should in future be based on the rating valuation. which in accordance with the Valuation for Rating Act, 1953, will be the June, 1939, rental value of the property in the state in which it exists at the time of valuation, or the current rental value, whichever is the lower.

213. We agree with the Majority that "It does not follow that what is fair as a measure of value for rating is equally fair as a measure of value for income tax. For one of the central problems of income tax is to relate to each other the taxable capacities of incomes of different kinds from different sources."[1] To express the income attritutable to the occupation of a house in terms of 1939 values, when the income from any other source is expressed in current values, amounts in our view to a discrimination in favour of a particular form of income.

[1] Para. 848.

214. We are also in agreement with the view that the existence of rent control makes it impossible to find a perfectly just solution of the problem. On the one hand, it seems unfair to charge the owner-occupier on the basis of current value when the occupier of an identical house, which is rent-controlled, is charged on the pre-war value. On the other hand it seems equally unfair to charge the occupier of a rented house built since the war on a post-war basis, whereas if he were an owner-occupier he would be charged (in effect) on a pre-war basis. Whatever the method chosen, it is possible to construct examples which imply unfairness between different taxpayers.

215. It must be borne in mind that the number of owner-occupied houses whose letting value is effectively tied to the pre-war rental (because (a) their rateable value is below the maxima specified in the Rent Acts, and (b) they have been let on or before September, 1939, or at a comparable rental afterwards) must be relatively small, and with the passage of time must become smaller still. We do not believe therefore that it would cause as much unfairness between owner-occupiers if the charge were based on the current letting value, as would be caused between owner-occupiers and others if the charge continued to be based on the pre-war value.

216. If the proposal for basing the charge on owner-occupiers on 1939 values for all houses (irrespective of whether they are pre-war or post-war built, and whether they are rent controlled or not) were accepted on a quasi-permanent basis the tax on owner-occupiers would become an arbitrary and an artificial one incapable of fulfilling the role for which it was originally designed. Since the difference between the nominal value and the true annual value would get steadily larger any subsequent attempt to remedy the situation would meet with resistance which would be the greater the longer the adjustment was delayed. We therefore prefer that irrespective of the basis of valuation adopted for rating purposes, the Schedule A charge should continue to be based on the rent for which a property is actually let, or the amount for which it is "worth to be let by the year" if it is not so let. This should be interpreted to mean that for houses which have acquired a "standard rent" under the Rent Control Acts up to August 30,

1954, the charge should be based on the standard rent; for other houses, it should be based on the current letting value. In order to prevent hardship arising from any sudden adjustment of the Schedule A charge we propose that the adjustment of the charge from the pre-war to the current value should proceed in gradual annual instalments, the increase not exceeding 10 per cent. of the existing charge in any one year. We recognise that this is not an ideal solution (since owner-occupiers with a "standard rent" under the Rent Control Acts would remain at an advantage in relation to other owner-occupiers) but at least it offers the prospect of gradually restoring the Schedule A charge to its original and equitable conception.

SUMMARY OF RECOMMENDATIONS

217. The following is a summary of our principal recommendations together with those of the Majority's recommendations which we wish to endorse and those from which we dissent.[1]

Capital Gains

(1) Capital gains of individuals should be subjected to income tax, but not to surtax (paragraph 62). Capital gains of companies should be charged to corporation profits tax (paragraph 107).

(2) The tax should be charged on the net realised gains of the year, after deduction of net realised losses. When net realised losses exceed net gains, the difference should be carried forward against future gains (paragraph 65).

(3) No distinction is to be made between short- and long-term gains. The transfer of property through inheritance or *inter vivos* gifts or settlements should reckon as realisation, the property being valued for the purpose by the same rules as are applicable to stamp duties (paragraphs 63, 64).

[1]Paragraph references are to the present Memorandum of Dissent. References to the Report are indicated by square brackets.

E

(4) Net unabsorbed capital losses shown by an estate at probate valuation should be credited against estate duty liabilities (paragraph 67).

(5) Net receipts from the sale of terminable rights (after deduction of any sum that may have been paid by the recipient for the acquisition of those rights) which are now exempt from tax should be subjected to income tax in an analogous manner to capital gains (paragraph 71).

(6) Gains arising on the sale of owner-occupied houses, to the extent of one residence for each taxpayer, should be exempt from the capital gains tax (paragraph 68).

(7) For the purpose of the first introduction of the tax assets purchased before the appointed day should, in the case of securities quoted on the Stock Exchange, be deemed to have been purchased at the middle price ruling on the appointed day; in the case of other assets, the actual cost of acquisition should reckon as the purchase price, but the taxable gain should be reduced to that fraction of the total gain which the period between the appointed day and the date of realisation bears to the total period of ownership (paragraph 69).

(8) For an initial period the tax should be limited to gains arising from the sale of businesses, securities of all kinds and real property, and there should be an exemption limit determined by administrative considerations (paragraph 70).

Corporate Taxation

(9) Company profits should be subject only to one tax—the corporation profits tax. No income tax should be levied on companies as such but companies should be asked to act as agents to the Revenue and deduct income tax at the ruling standard rate from all interest and dividends paid out (paragraph 92).

(10) Simultaneously with the introduction of the capital gains tax the existing discrimination between distributed and undistributed profits should be abolished and companies should be charged at the uniform rate to corporation

profits tax on the whole of their profits (paragraph 106).

(11) Income tax deducted at source on the interest and dividends, etc., received by corporations should be credited against the corporation profits tax liability (paragraph 106).

(12) 33⅓ per cent. should be regarded as the appropriate rate for the tax on corporate profits at the present level of taxation, and in the light of the charge to be imposed on capital gains. The tax should initially be charged at 40 per cent., which is the equivalent rate of the present taxes falling on corporations, but the rate should subsequently be reduced as an offset to the revenue from the newly imposed tax on capital gains until it is reduced to 33⅓ per cent. (paragraphs 108–109).

Earned Income Relief

(13) Earned income relief should be available to incomes assessed under Schedule E without any upper income limit (paragraph 129 (i)).

(14) In the case of individuals and partnerships assessed under Case II of Schedule D earned income relief should be available without any upper limit but only to taxpayers who are at their own option assessed on their profits under the Schedule E expenses rule (paragraph 129 (ii)).

(15) In the case of unincorporated businesses assessed under Case I of Schedule D, earned income relief should be available up to the limits recommended in paragraph 220 of the Second Report of the Royal Commission but only to taxpayers who are at their own option assessed on their profits under the Schedule E expenses rule (paragraph 129 (iii)).

(16) Taxpayers with incomes assessed under Cases I and II of Schedule D, exercising the option to be assessed under the Schedule E expenses rule, should not be able to claim such expenses as are (*a*) not of a capital nature and (*b*) not directly and inevitably involved in earning the profits of the year (paragraph 129 (iv)).

Relief for Losses

   (17) Apart from financial concerns, to which the provisions of the Income Tax Act, 1952, Section 342 (4), should continue to apply, losses in future should be offset only against future income from the same source (paragraph 142).

   (18) Until the introduction of the capital gains tax financial concerns which are taxed on their capital gains as dealers in securities should be able to offset losses arising out of security transactions only against future gains from the same source (paragraph 147).

   (19) Companies which are able to deduct, as expenses, payments made to subsidiary companies under the provisions of the Finance Act, 1953, Section 20, should not be able to claim such deductions in cases where the payments are made to a subsidiary acquired by the parent company in the knowledge that it was incurring losses (paragraph 146).

Capital Allowances

   (20) Simultaneously with the introduction of a tax on the receipts from the sale of terminable rights (paragraph 71) we recommend the introduction of a capital allowance (subject to a balancing charge) for the cost of mineral rights and for the premiums paid on leases (paragraph 149).

   (21) The treatment of capital allowances given to agriculture should be assimilated to the treatment of capital allowances generally (paragraph 151).

Stock Valuation

   (22) Valuation by the "first-in-first-out" method should be the general rule for valuing stocks in the ascertainment of trading profits for tax purposes. Departures from this rule should be granted only (*a*) in cases where the actual cost incurred in connection with any particular item sold can be directly ascertained; (*b*) with the consent of the Revenue authorities in those cases where a business

cannot reasonably be expected to keep the records necessary for the ascertainment of stocks by this method and a simpler method of stock valuation is regarded as adequate; (c) when current market value is below actual cost, valuation on the basis of market value should be permitted at the option of the taxpayer (paragraphs 158, 160).

Double Taxation Relief
(23) Relief given to individuals with respect to foreign taxation should be limited to the tax so imposed on individuals and relief given to companies should be limited to the corresponding taxes imposed on companies (paragraph 172).

Expense Allowances and Benefits in Kind
(24) The Board of Inland Revenue should publish annually in their Report figures relating to the operation of the 1948 legislation showing (i) the number of cases in which assessments were raised as a result of the operation of the Act; (ii) the total amount of expenses claimed in these cases; (iii) the amount of such expenses that were disallowed (paragraph 189).

Superannuation
(25) Relief should be extended on the lines recommended by the second Tucker Committee with the exception of the self-employed and controlling directors. Taxpayers assessed under Case II of Schedule D should be permitted through their professional associations to organise and administer superannuation funds on analogous lines to those set up under the Finance Act, 1921, Section 32 (paragraph 196).
(26) Lump-sum benefits should be abolished in the case of all future entrants to superannuation schemes without prejudice to existing members of such schemes (paragraph 199).

Covenants
(27) A review ought to be undertaken of the present system of

inheritance taxes in connection with the question of income and property transfers generally; and the question of the tax treatment of voluntary transfers of income by means of covenants should form part of such an inquiry (paragraph 208).

(28) As an interim measure the amount of convenanted income the transfer of which is recognised for the purpose of surtax assessment of the covenantor, should be limited to £500 a year in the case of any one beneficiary (paragraph 210).

Charities

(29) There should be a more restrictive definition of a charity for tax purposes and charities should only receive tax exemption up to a certain rate of income tax and only at half the rate for any excess (paragraph 211).

Schedule A Charge on Dwelling-houses

(30) The charge should continue to be based on the rent for which a property is actually let or the amount for which it is worth to be let by the year if it is not so let. The amount for "which it is worth to be let by the year" should be interpreted as the amount of the "standard rent" for houses which have acquired a "standard rent" under the Rent Control Acts prior to August 30th, 1954, and for other houses it should be based on the current letting value. In order to prevent hardship the adjustment of the Schedule A charge on owner-occupiers from the pre-war to the current value should proceed in gradual instalments, the increases not exceeding 10 per cent. of the existing charge in any one year (paragraph 216).

MAJORITY RECOMMENDATIONS

We should like to endorse the following principal recommendations of the Majority:

A. RECOMMENDATIONS REFERRED TO IN THE MEMORANDUM

Capital Allowances
(31) Capital allowances should be given for commercial buildings; surpluses realised on the sale of assets qualifying for capital allowances should be subject to tax except in the case of ships built before 1946; cutting and tunnelling work should qualify for annual and balancing allowances (paragraphs 149, 151).

Personal expenses
(32) Directors or employees of charitable bodies or non-trading concerns should be subject to the special legislation dating from 1948 (paragraph 188).

Compensation for Loss of Office, etc.
(33) Payment for compensation for loss of office should be taxable. The whole of such payments, as well as ex gratia payments on termination of service should be charged (paragraphs 200–201).

Covenants
(34) Covenants for the purpose of discretionary trusts should be rendered ineffective for tax purposes (paragraph 209).
(35) The maker of a covenant in favour of a family member should be required to produce each year formal declarations by himself and the beneficiary as to the absence of any agreement or understanding for the return, direct or indirect, of any part of the benefit. This should be extended to all relatives and the declaration required should be on oath (paragraph 209).

B. RECOMMENDATIONS NOT PREVIOUSLY REFERRED TO

(36) Relief for fluctuating incomes and consequent repeal of special provisions concerning authors [paragraphs 203, 207].

(37) A director should be entitled to the same benefit as an employee in respect of living accommodation [paragraph 219 (2)].

(38) Special relief for travelling costs occasioned by war circumstances should be terminated [paragraph 237].

(39) In the case of multiple employment, relief should be given for travelling between the principal place of work and the place where the subsidiary calling is excercised [paragraph 241].

(40) Post-cessation receipts should be taxable [paragraphs 262, 264].

(41) Rules concerning residence, ordinary residence and foreign employment should be rationalised and codified [paragraphs 293–307].

(42) Bad debt recoveries should be taxable [paragraph 265].

(43) Payments for the hire or use of an asset should be deductible in computing profits and taxed in the hands of the recipient [paragraph 404].

(44) Surpluses of corporations engaged in mutual trading should be taxable [paragraph 593].

(45) The B.B.C. should be exempt from income tax and profits tax on its trading profit [paragraph 601].

(46) Schedule D tax should be assessed on a current year basis for companies under Cases I and II and for all taxpayers under Cases IV and V [paragraphs 776, 789].

(47) Nationalised and public utility undertakings should be taxed on the same basis as other concerns [paragraphs 567, 569].

(48) Industrial and provident societies and building societies should be taxed only on the retained balance of profits [paragraphs 573, 577].

(49) Bonus debentures should be sur-taxable [paragraph 800].

(50) Dividends paid out of capital profits should be taxable [paragraph 808].

(51) Recommendations concerning Schedules A and B with the exception of the suggested basis of charge for the owner-occupier [paragraphs 838–926]; Administration [paragraphs 948–1012]; Tax Avoidance [paragraphs 1029–1047] and Tax Evasion [paragraphs 1052–1089].

DISSENTS

We wish to dissent from the following principal recommendations in the Report:

(52) Immediate abolition of the discriminatory tax on distributed profits (paragraph 105).

(53) Amendment of the Schedule E expenses rule (paragraph 122).

(54) Statutory disavowal of Lord Davey's test (paragraph 113).

(55) Relief for unexhausted capital allowances and investment allowances against other income for any future year (paragraph 145).

(56) Permission to use the L.I.F.O. method of stock valuation for tax purposes (paragraph 161).

(57) Extension of double taxation relief to provincial, canton, and municipal taxes irrespective of existing limitations (paragraph 171).

(58) Relief from foreign "indirect tax" to be given to a minority shareholder irrespective of existing limitations (paragraph 170).

(59) Introduction of a special category of "overseas trade corporation" to be exempt from tax (paragraph 179).

(60) Abolition of special rule concerning expenses and benefits in kind for non-controlling directors receiving less than £2,000 a year (paragraph 185).

(61) Abandonment of the attempt to take into account "home savings" (paragraph 187).

CONCLUDING STATEMENT

218. These are our recommendations for a reform of the existing system of income and profits taxation. We have made no attempt to estimate the resulting net balance but there is no doubt that their adoption would increase the revenue. We do not therefore feel called upon to lay down a list of priorities. We wish, however, to record our opinion that if these reforms were adopted, and the basis of taxation were thus brought into closer conformity with the true taxable capacity of different classes of taxpayers, there would be a strong case for adopting a more moderate scale of progression in the schedule of tax rates. Our present schedule of rates (perhaps through a process of instinctive judgment on the part of legislators, rather than through deliberate intent) tends to take account of the fact that the tax base lags increasingly behind true taxable capacity as we move up the income scale—just as in some other countries, where tax evasion is prevalent, evasion leads to higher nominal rates which in turn lead to further evasion and still higher rates. The adoption of a more comprehensive definition of income as the tax base would be a great deal easier—imposing fewer strains on the social fabric and on the administration of the tax system—if it were accompanied by a more moderate rate schedule; and this would nevertheless inaugurate a more truly progressive and equitable system of taxation.

2

A PROPOSAL FOR A LEVY ON THE ADVERTISING REVENUE OF NEWSPAPERS[1]

1. The purpose of this memorandum is to advocate special measures to counteract the tendency to concentration in the newspaper industry. Measures are needed because Britain suffers a growing concentration of the popular daily Press in the hands of a few newspaper owners. This is depriving the public of the variety of independent views and sources of information essential for the sustenance of a vigorous and alert public opinion, without which democratic institutions cannot function effectively.

2. In this memorandum the case is set out with reference to national newspapers only. Much of the argument applies to other parts of the Press as well—particularly to the chains of provincial newspapers—and we believe that similar measures could be devised for application there.

The Trend Towards Monopoly

3. In any industry where fixed costs are large in relation to variable costs, there are economies of large-scale production which cause a competitive market to be unstable: once particular producers obtain a lead over their rivals, they are able to enhance that lead until one or a few of them dominate the market. Stability in competition in an industry requires that there should be an optimum size for a firm (a size beyond which further expansion causes an increase in costs), which is none too large in relation to the whole industry. But in the long run the only factor capable of imposing a check on the expansion of an individual business, in the form of higher relative costs, is the diseconomies of

[1] Memorandum submitted jointly with R. R. Neild to the Royal Commission on the Press, February 1962.

large-scale management; such diseconomies, however, are only significant in those particular industries (such as agriculture) where the very increase in the scale of operations involves a multiplication of day-to-day decisions of the kind which cannot effectively be delegated. This is *not* the case in the newspaper industry, where the important day-to-day decisions—those concerning editorial content and policy—are virtually independent of the size of circulation. The newspaper industry is therefore *par excellence* one in which increasing returns prevail virtually without limit.

4. In most industries the tendency to monopoly is checked, sooner or later, by one or both of two factors (other than the diseconomies of large-scale management). The first is that beyond a certain point the cost advantages of further increases in scale become insignificant: there is a limit beyond which the further spreading of overheads yields only negligible reductions in unit costs. Secondly, the lack of unity of the market—due to locational differences, special advantages, or simply the force of habit or the inertia of buyers—limit the extent to which any one producer can appropriate to himself the share of the market belonging to his rivals by under-cutting them.

5. But in modern industries, subject to long-run economies of scale, businesses have two additional weapons at their disposal with which to increase their command of the market beyond the point to which it could be carried by the weapon of price competition alone. One is product variation and the other is advertising and related forms of sales-promotion. A producer who obtains a lead over his rivals and so has lower costs and makes a larger profit, need not cut his prices in order to expand his share of the market. He can commonly achieve his aim more safely and more effectively by making additional outlays with the purpose of increasing his sales at prices which are not out of line with those charged by other producers. Such outlays may be devoted either to the introduction of additional, non-optional features in his product, designed to make it more attractive to buyers (for example, more chrome on motor cars) or they may be devoted to large-scale advertising of the product and to promotional campaings (for example, gift-coupons, competitions,

prizes, etc.). While there is an apparent difference between these two types of outlay, they are alike in their purpose and their effect: their purpose is to enhance sales; their effect is to raise the utility of the product to the buyer by less than the extra costs incurred. It is important to emphasise—because the contrary is so often asserted by interested parties—that the fact that it serves to enlarge the producer's profit creates no presumption that such expenditure on sales promotion, whether associated with so-called "quality improvements" or not, has been incurred *in deference to* consumers' preferences. For the common feature of situations in which such expenditures are undertaken is that the consumer is not free to decide whether, and how far, he will pay for such additional outlays. The producer who obtains an advantage over rivals in the form of lower costs, generally does not offer the consumer the original product at a reduced price as an alternative to paying the old price for the "improved" or heavily advertised product.

6. One important consequence of the process of industrial concentration is that it leads to a much higher degree of standardisation in production than would be possible otherwise. This permits the exploitation of techniques of mass production which, as America first demonstrated to the world, can bring very important benefits in the form of higher productivity and living standards. But it necessarily involves the sacrifice of minority tastes and interests for the sake of the better satisfaction of the majority. It is of course inevitable that the range of things actually produced should represent a small selection from the almost infinite variety that would have to be produced if everybody's individual tastes were separately catered for. However, under the modern regime of mass production, standardisation is carried to a point where the specification of things produced is the result of careful researches into the "highest common factor" in the tastes of the average consumer in the community. This in turn induces a uniformity of tastes and habits, since people's tastes and interests are themselves strongly influenced by what is put before them. In most fields—for example, housing, food, clothing or transport—we are ready to accept the loss of the flavour of life, caused by this imposed uniformity, for the sake of the freedom

gained through higher living standards. But it is generally recognised that when it comes to the satisfaction of intellectual needs, the standardisation of what is put before the public, and the neglect of individual tastes and interests, inevitably leads to the degeneration of society. No one would argue that a large reduction in the number of novels, plays or scientific books that is produced would be justified for the sake of the economies of mass production.

Special Features of the Newspaper Industry

7. There are two special features of the newspaper industry which make the tendencies to concentration, caused by the economies of mass production and the modern methods of non-price competition, operate more powerfully here than in other industries or in other sectors of the publishing industry.

(i) Upward pressure on overheads

The first is that in the newspaper industry expenditure on "quality improvement" involves a higher expenditure on overhead or *fixed costs*, and not (or not necessarily) on higher variable costs. The producer who has an initial lead can outbid his rivals by devoting his extra profits to forms of expenditure that increase the appeal of his paper—employing large numbers of reporters to pick up the latest news or gossip; spending more on "feature" articles; maintaining a large staff of foreign correspondents; and (last but not least) employing a correspondingly large and highly paid staff to sift, and present in the most appealing form, a diminishing proportion of the material gathered for publication. All this increases the ratio of fixed to variable costs *for any given circulation* and thereby renews the economic advantages of large-scale production which would otherwise have petered out as circulation rose. In the technical jargon of economists, the curve of overhead costs is raised and shifted to the right so as to make the "break-even point" higher, and the cost advantages of further increases of circulation greater, as circulations are increased.[1]

---

[1] The implications of this tendency can be shown by means of a simple diagram. Let circulation be measured along OX, and the costs per copy and the price along

These aggressive techniques of non-price competition (which force a progressive increase in the break-even point at any *given* price) have generally proved far more potent in eliminating rivals, both in the newspaper industry and elsewhere, than price competition. In manufacturing industry similar results arise

OY. Let us assume, for simplicity, that variable costs (newsprint, ink, etc.) are proportionate to circulation, whereas editorial and management costs are independent of circulation. Let the line CC^1. represent variable costs per unit, and a series of rectangular hyperbolae, f^1, f^2 ... (added to CC^1) the fixed costs per unit as determined by "editorial" expenditure. If the price per copy is P and fixed costs are f^1, the minimum circulation required to cover costs is M.

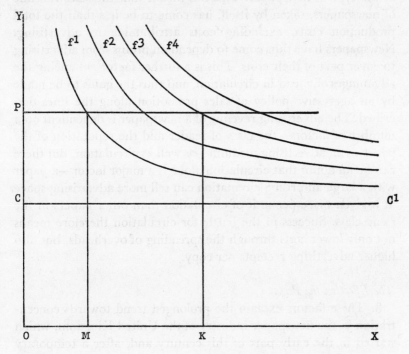

Suppose a newspaper achieves a circulation K, which enables it to increase fixed costs to f^3, which in turn forces other newspapers to try to follow suit, so that fixed costs for the average paper are raised to f^2. Since the paper incurring f^3 costs has now an additional sales appeal, its circulation increases further, thereby making it possible to increase the scale of fixed costs to, say, f^4. This in turn forces other papers to increase their fixed costs and will cause some of them (who cannot afford sufficient additional expenditure) to fall by the wayside. In the course of this process the "break-even point" (i.e. the minimum circulation necessary to cover total costs) is continually pushed up, whilst the relative advantage of the most successful paper, represented by the difference in fixed costs which it can afford to incur and those which the others can afford to incur, becomes steadily greater.

because the most successful firms incur advertising expenditure
on a much greater scale than their smaller rivals.

(ii) *Advertising*

The second special feature which enhances the advantages of
large newspaper circulations is advertising. With the growth of
modern advertising, the price and cost structure of the newspaper industry has been gradually shifted in such a way that the
sales revenue of newspapers has come to represent the smaller
part, and advertising revenue the larger part, of the total receipts
of the typical newspaper. This has meant that the sales revenue
of newspapers, taken by itself, has come to be less than the total
production costs, excluding costs attributable to advertising.
Newspapers have thus come to depend on profits from advertising
to cover part of their costs. This is a further factor enhancing the
advantages of a lead in circulation, and thus the gains to be made
by an aggressive policy of sales promotion along the lines described. The advertising revenue of a newspaper is dependent on a
number of factors—the class of reader and the reputation of the
paper as an advertising medium—as well as circulation. But there
can be no doubt that circulation alone is a major factor—a paper
with a large and rising circulation can sell more advertising space
at a given price per unit of circulation than other papers in the
same class. Success in the battle for circulation therefore means
not only lower costs through the spreading of overheads, but also
higher advertising receipts per copy.

The Effect on the Press

8. These factors explain the prolonged trend towards concentration in the newspaper industry of the United Kingdom, which
started in the early part of this century and, after a temporary
lull, has once again shown its force recently. In the course of this
process the popular paper of mass appeal has become increasingly
divorced from the type of newspaper mainly devoted to a straight
presentation of news and opinion. Papers of the latter type (now
called the "quality papers") have been reduced to a very small
number, each of limited circulation. The battle for circulation
has forced the others to concentrate more and more on crude

sensationalism (crime, sex, social gossip), leaving less and less space for the straight presentation of national or international affairs. Despite the efforts of rival popular papers to conform to the same pattern, the process of non-price competition has forced a succession of papers out of business. The point has now been reached where the number of popular daily morning papers of a national circulation has been reduced to five (excluding the *Daily Telegraph* which manages to preserve a special role astride the two classes), at least two of which face an uncertain future. The probability that anyone will break into the newspaper industry is extremely small; indeed the *News Chronicle* went under when it had a circulation of over a million. The large and artificially swollen "break-even point" makes the cost of entry prohibitive and this endows the established papers with a privileged position akin to that enjoyed in earlier times by monopolies established by royal charter.

9. For reasons argued above, we regard this situation as contrary to the public interest and sufficiently important to justify the introduction of special measures to counteract and reverse the trend towards monopoly. We do not believe, for reasons explained in para. 5, that there is any presumption in favour of the view that the present character of the popular Press, and the very limited choice of papers, is an expression of the general will as registered by the preferences of the public; and we feel that it is wholly illegitimate to adduce the operation of market forces in favour of any such presumption. In monopolistic situations it cannot be asserted that the free play of market forces produces results that are in accord with consumers' preferences taken individually. Moreover, in the case of the newspaper industry there are important social and political considerations in favour of a varied and competitive industry which are distinct from, and additional to, considerations relating to the efficient satisfaction of individual preferences. We do not believe that the vast editorial outlays of the mammoth papers yield true benefits of any significance to the readers, let alone sufficient benefit to outweigh the very serious harm caused by the lack of newspapers capable of giving expression to a variety of points of view, and of providing a fuller and more unbiased presentation of news.

Remedies

10. Any effective remedy must make large circulations less profitable relative to smaller ones, and reduce the size that a paper must achieve if it is to stay in business (i.e. reduce the "break-even point"). The most convenient instrument for this purpose is a levy graduated so as to increase the effective cost to the publisher when circulation increases beyond a certain figure, combined with an equalisation payment which has the effect of raising the proportion of revenue that is directly geared to sales. We therefore propose that a levy should be imposed on the newspaper industry, the proceeds of which are returned to the industry in such a way that the net result is to change the relative profitability of small and large circulations. Since advertising revenue is a kind of bounty to newspapers, which arises from performing a service which is incidental to their functions as newspapers and bears little relation to the cost of providing that service, the most reasonable method of achieving this end is to impose a levy on revenue from advertising; the rate of the levy as a percentage of (gross) advertising revenue should be graduated according to circulation, and there should be total exemption for newspapers whose circulation is below a minimum level. The following schedule is constructed as illustration; we do not have the information necessary to calculate what in practice would be the appropriate schedule.

NATIONAL DAILY MORNING NEWSPAPERS

Circulation	Rate of levy on Gross Revenue from Advertising
The first 500,000	nil
500,000–1 million	7·5 per cent.
1 million–2 million	20 per cent.
2 million–3 million	40 per cent.
Above 3 million	50 per cent.

11. In order to avoid large jumps in the liability when certain circulation levels are reached, we suggest that the actual schedule should be broken down into a larger number of small steps. In the above example, the actual schedule might be stated in terms

of an increase of 1 per cent. for every 50,000 of circulation, or an increase of 2 per cent. for every 100,000 of circulation, above the level of 500,000. In order to prevent people from evading the levy by producing the same newspaper under a variety of titles, we suggest that papers should be identified by reference to their ownership and contents (excluding advertising)—papers with two titles being regarded as the same newspaper if more than, say, 60 per cent. of their editorial content is the same. We propose that the proceeds of the levy should be returned to the papers embraced in the scheme in the form of a flat rate equalisation payment of so much per copy sold, subject to a limit of, say, 2 million copies per day. Thus, supposing that the levy were to yield £10 million per annum, and the total circulation of newspapers (excluding that part of the circulations which is in excess of 2 million per day) is 10 million copies per day, the equalisation payment would be £1 a year per copy, or approximately 0·8d. per copy per day, subject to a maximum payment of £6,667 per day, or £2 million a year, for any one paper.

12. No doubt a proposal of this kind would be heavily criticised by interested parties as an interference with "freedom" and as a scheme which "penalises the strong in order to support the weak". We should like to emphasise again that in this field, more than in any other, commercial success is no criterion of public advantage. It is well established that it is the duty of the State in a free society to take whatever steps are necessary and appropriate to keep the market free, and to check the aggregation of monopoly power which itself constitutes a menace to freedom. In the newspaper industry such aggregation of monopoly power has far worse consequences than in other fields, implying as it does a dictatorship over the sources of knowledge, accompanied by irresponsible power to condition the mind and to sway opinion. The Royal Commission on the Press of 1947–48 stated in its Conclusions (para. 674) that "any further decrease in the number of national newspapers would be a matter for anxiety". Since that time the number of national newspapers has decreased further. Indeed, it was the public anxiety created by the disappearance of an important newspaper last year which led to the appointment of the present Royal Commission. The time for action has arrived.

3

THE ECONOMIC EFFECTS OF ALTERNATIVE
SYSTEMS OF CORPORATION TAX[1]

THE purpose of this memorandum is to examine the economic
and social effects of various alternative systems of company
taxation. Though the Select Committee's terms of reference
explicitly ask for consideration of one of two alternative systems
described in the Green Paper (Cmnd. 4630)—the so-called "two-
rate system" and the "imputation system"—it would be impossible (in my view) to consider their economic effects without comparing these with other alternatives, such as the retention of the
existing system of corporation tax. This is important also in
view of the fact that the recommendations of the van der Tempel
report clearly suggest that system (described in the report as
the "classical system") in preference to the others for purposes
of tax harmonisation in the Community so that it may be necessary to retain, or to return to, that system if the U.K. entered the
Common Market.

The main reason advanced by the Government for a reform
of the present system is that it entails "a discrimination in favour
of retained as opposed to distributed profits" and this "discrimination distorts the working of market forces and so tends
towards the misallocation of scarce investment resources".[2]

The purpose of this paper is to argue, on the contrary, that the
present system of corporate taxation is more conducive to both
investment and an efficient allocation of resources than either
of the two variants proposed in the Green Paper.

To demonstrate this it is necessary to compare the various

---

[1] Memorandum submitted to the Select Committee of the House of Commons on the
Corporation Tax, July 1971.
[2] "Budget Statement", *Hansard*, 30 March 1971, col. 1383.

systems with the rates of taxation so adjusted as to yield the same revenue to the Exchequer. Thus the Green Paper suggests (for illustrative purposes) a rate of corporation tax of 50 per cent. and distribution relief of 30 per cent. The proposed revenue yield of a 50 per cent. corporation tax with 30 per cent. distribution relief may be no greater than that of a 29 per cent. corporation tax without distribution relief.[1] Alternatively, it might require a rate of tax of 61 per cent. to produce, in combination with a 30 per cent. distribution relief, the same yield as the present corporation tax at the rate of 40 per cent.

Since it is always open to the Government to alleviate the burden of taxation falling on companies by reducing the *rates* of taxation (the present Government has already reduced the rates of Corporation Tax from 45 per cent. to 40 per cent. and there is no reason, other than the need for revenue, why it should not reduce it further) the only meaningful comparison between the present and the proposed systems is on the assumption that the new system involves an appropriately higher rate of taxation than the present one. Assuming that the new tax will be introduced at a 50 per cent. rate, the question to be considered therefore is whether the proposed tax is superior in its economic effects to the present "discriminating" tax at the rate, not of 50 per cent. but say, of 30–35 per cent.

Arguments Against the Proposed Reforms

Looked at in this way the proposed system can be shown to suffer from three major disadvantages in comparison with the existing system:

(1) It involves considerably higher *marginal* rates of taxation;

---

[1] Suppose a company makes a taxable profit of 100, pays corporation tax of 40, and of the remainder, it distributes 42 and retains 18. Under the new system the company *could* distribute 70 and retain 30 *before tax*; in that case its total tax charge would come to 29 per cent. (20 per cent. on 70 plus 50 per cent. on 30) which would leave it with a net retention of only 1. A more reasonable supposition would be that the company under the new system would still wish to retain, say, 10 (instead of 18 as at present) and distribute whatever is left after paying corporation tax: in that case it could distribute 56, on which it would get distribution relief of 30 per cent., i.e. 16·8; so that its total tax charge would come to *33·2 per cent.*, which would leave it with a net retained profit of 10·8. By the same token, a company wishing to retain 15 would pay at an effective rate of *35 per cent.*, and have 50 available for distribution. Finally, if the company wished to retain the *same* amount net under the new system as the old (an "extreme case") the tax charge would come to *36·3 per cent.*

this is alone relevant from the point of view of the inducement to invest. For it is only in the case of marginal investments (i.e. investments near the margin of profitability) that the disincentive effects of taxation become important for business decisions. Projects which are well within the margin of profitability are not likely to be affected one way or another either by the disincentive effects of taxation or the incentive effects of investment grants, accelerated depreciation, etc. And for marginal investment it is the *marginal* rate of taxation which matters. Whatever criteria businesses use for determining a "cut-off point" for investment (whether it is a target rate of return, or a pay-off period) rational decision requires that the "target" should be calculated on a net-of-tax basis. For example, if a business uses a target rate of return (after amortisation) of say, 10 per cent. net of corporation tax, the return before tax must exceed 10 per cent. by $1/1-t$, where t is the marginal rate of taxation. When the marginal rate is 50 per cent. this means that the expected return before tax must be 20 per cent. for the project to qualify for adoption; if the marginal rate is $33\frac{1}{3}$ per cent., the expected return need only be 15 per cent.

(2) The proposal involves a redistribution in the burden of taxation between companies; companies with a high share of retained profits will pay *more* under the new system, whilst companies which distribute a high proportion of their profits will pay *less*. As far as publicly quoted companies are concerned (and these account for much the greater proportion of business investment) there is a close correlation (at least over a run of years) between the amount of retained profits and the level of investment. Publicly quoted companies (and particularly companies with widespread ownership) do not retain profits which are not required for business expansion. The profit which they retain is essential in order to ensure the growth of the business over longer periods; it is naïve to suppose that a growing company can finance its long-term requirements by continued borrowing or continued share issues in *substitution* of retentions. A fast growing company will need both internal and external finance: the two are *complementary* to each other and not substitutes. The amount a company is able to raise externally—by way of bank loans or debentures *or* by way of rights issues—is itself related to the growth of

its own reserves. All that a well developed financial system is able to accomplish is to raise the proportion of external "matching finance" which is available to a firm as a supplement to its internal savings. Without a developed capital market a company can only raise money in the form of short- or long-term loans; the extent of this is always limited by the collateral it can offer and such finance cannot exceed a certain proportion of total assets. Assuming that this proportion is reached (i.e., assuming that a certain debt/asset ratio is attained) any further borrowing requires a corresponding addition to owned reserves. If we suppose, e.g., that a debt/asset ratio of over 50 per cent. is regarded as suspect, this means that a company cannot safely reckon, over a run of years, to raise external finance for more than one-third of its total financial requirements. For each £ ploughed back, its borrowing power will expand by 50p. Clearly the more it can plough back, the more it can borrow.

It is not as clearly understood that the situation remains essentially the same even in an economy with a highly developed capital market (such as the U.K.) where it is possible to raise money as a regular matter in the form of issues of ordinary shares for cash, and not only by way of borrowing. It still remains true that the amount that can be raised by new issues, over a longer period is—in a rather more complex fashion—dependent on, and related to, the growth of internal reserves. The main reason for this is that in a world of uncertainty, the record of past growth is the main consideration in the choice of securities in the minds of portfolio investors and investment managers, as is shown by the fact that the price/earnings ratio in the case of "growth stocks"—i.e. in the case of companies whose earnings and dividends *per share* have been rising over time—tends to exceed by a considerable margin the price/earnings ratio of non-growth stocks. This means also that "growth stocks" (i.e. companies with a record of rising earnings and dividends by share) will have a higher "valuation ratio" *in relation* to the rate of return on the capital employed than non-growth stocks. The "valuation ratio" is defined as the ratio of the market capitalisation of the company in relation to the capital actually employed by it (or the ratio of the market value per share to net assets per share). It is this "valuation ratio" (and not just the price/earnings ratio) which determines the terms on which (and the ease with which) a company can obtain finance through the issue of new equity capital. Suppose this valuation ratio is 2 (which means each share has twice the value of the [fixed and current] assets it represents) a company can double the amount of capital at the disposal of the business by a rights issue of around 1 for 2. But if the valuation ratio is 5, the same addition to its financial resources would only require a rights issue of 1 to 5. In the second case the "effective cost" of raising money through new equity issues is much smaller than in the first case.

The "valuation ratio" of a company will partly depend on the rate of return on the capital employed, and partly on how fast the return per share has been rising over time. Other things being equal, the more earnings and dividends per share are rising over time the higher will the market price of a company's share be both in relation to assets per share and in relation to earnings. Rising earnings and dividends per share can only be ensured (whatever the rate of profitability of investments) if *some* part of the growth in capital employed is financed by retentions.

This preference for "growth stocks" is partly a consequence of differences in the effective rates of taxation between dividend income and capital appreciation—a difference which is not *predominantly* the consequence of higher marginal rates of income tax and surtax on dividend income as against the rate of capital gains tax, but of the fact that income tax is paid *simultaneously* with the receipt of the dividend, whereas capital gains tax is typically only paid some years *after* the appreciation has occurred, when the gains are "realised". It is partly also a reflection of more basic factors arising from the general expectation that the trend of money incomes and prices is more likely to be rising than falling over time. Growth stocks are preferred by tax-exempt investors (such as charities or pension funds) and not only by tax-paying investors mainly because they feel "safer" with growth stocks in times of inflation. This is best shown by the general aversion to investment in bonds and preference shares by charities and pension funds, despite the relatively high yield obtainable on such securities in relation to ordinary shares. And it must be emphasised that in times of inflation a company which distributes the whole of its earnings after depreciation is in a far more vulnerable position for maintaining the *real value* of the dividend to its shareholders than a company which increases the money value of the assets per share through a regular addition to its reserves.

This explains why a company's ability to raise money in the capital market depends not only on the current and prospective return on the capital employed but also on the rate of growth of its sales and its profits. As Henderson and Tew had shown in their well-known study[1] only the hundred fastest-growing companies had regular access to the London capital market by way of rights issues in the 1950s, and these companies have invariably also retained a *high* proportion of their current earnings, despite their ability to have regular recourse to external equity finance. For these highly successful companies it was undoubtedly true that thanks to the capital market they were able to expand at a faster rate than they could have done on the basis of retained profits alone, even if they had retained the whole of their earnings. But it is equally true that such "regular access to the capital market" presupposes that *some* proportion of the growth of finance comes from retentions—i.e. that "internal" and "external" sources of finance are complements to each other, and not alternatives. The conclusion which emerges from these studies (and which can be well supported also by general theoretical considerations) is that for highly profitable and fast expanding companies there is an optimal "retention ratio" of profits which maximises their "valuation ratio" at any given rate of return (and hence the price/earnings ratio) and which therefore maximises the rate at which a company can increase the growth of financial resources at its command, taking both internal and external sources into account.

A more recent study by Singh and Whittington[2] has also shown that the fastest growing companies in the U.K. (in terms of sales or turnover) were also those which tended to earn the highest rates of return on the capital employed at any one time, and which had the highest rate of growth of capital employed, and these in

[1] R. F. Henderson and B. H. Tew, *Studies in Company Finance*, Cambridge University Press, 1959.
[2] A. Singh and G. Whittington, *Growth, Profitability and Valuation*, Cambridge University Press, 1968, pp. 179–180.

turn were companies which (whether they resorted to raising money by way of rights issues or not) also had the highest "retention ratios"—i.e. the largest share of current earnings ploughed back into the business. These conclusions are *not* inconsistent with I. M. D. Little's findings[1] that only a small proportion of the "successful" companies (as measured over, say, a five-year period) manage to keep up a record of exceptional growth over longer periods; and that in consequence, a great deal of the profits retained by businesses will not be found to have added to earnings as much as the rate of earnings on the capital employed at the time of fast growth and heavy retentions. The fact that the firms which grow fast are those which retain and invest a high proportion of their earnings does not imply that all firms which retain and invest more than the average will succeed in maintaining above average earnings and growth rates. To suggest that the successful companies have all been high retainers does not mean that all companies will be successful merely *because* they are high retainers.

But the point is that for a successful company high retentions are essential in order to exploit its growth-potential; and the less is taken from it in taxation, the faster it can grow at any given rate of return. For such a company a system which taxes retained profits at a higher rate obviously imposes a more stringent financial limitation on the attainable rate of expansion than an alternative system involving a lower rate of tax. The proposed reform of the Corporation Tax which redistributes the burden of taxation between companies in favour of the high distributors will thus necessarily cause the fastest-growing companies to be more severely handicapped by financial limitation; it will thereby reduce both the volume and the quality of business investment at any given level of business taxation.

(3) The third reason why the proposed reform of company taxation will have adverse socio-economic effects is connected with the effects of the change on consumption and savings. A change in the tax system favouring distributions and penalising retentions is bound to increase the volume of shareholders' consumption at any given level of post-corporation-tax profits.

[1] I. M. D. Little and A. C. Rayner, *Higgeldy Piggeldy Growth Again*, Oxford, Basil Blackwell, 1966.

This is because the propensity to consume out of dividend income is normally considerably higher than the propensity to consume out of (realised or unrealised) capital gains. Hence as more dividends are paid out and capital appreciation is reduced, shareholders' consumption at any given level of share values or company earnings is bound to increase. This means that under a full employment policy—where fiscal and monetary policy is governed by the desire "to deploy [manpower and other] resources to the maximum benefit"[1] more taxation will have to be imposed if an excessive pressure of demand is to be avoided; the higher propensity to consume by shareholders will have to be balanced by lower consumption (of all classes) achieved through higher taxation and thus a lower deficit (or higher surplus) on the consolidated account of public sector. This is only another way of saying that the new form of Corporation Tax has a lesser degree of "economic efficiency" than the exisitng form, and therefore requires a higher total to be raised in taxes of all kinds if the overall equilibrium of the economy is to be preserved. Given the succcessful pursuit of full employment policy, it would be wrong to say that total investment or savings will necessarily be *lower* in consequence, since budgetary policy will have to be adjusted so as to secure the same rate of growth of the G.D.P., if full employment is to be preserved, and this in turn may entail the same ratio of investment to the G.D.P. Hence, given "appropriate economic policies" which the present Government regards as "mandatory upon the United Kingdom in any event",[2] and assuming that in pursuance of this policy, the natural growth-potential of the economy is to be fully exploited, national savings, as a proportion of national income should be the same. But with less efficient tax instruments, the total level of taxation would have to be higher in relation to public expenditure; hence, for a given volume of national investment and savings, net public savings will be greater and net private savings less, than under the alternative system.

But this means that, despite its superficial attractions, the proposed reform of Corporation Tax besides being inimical to

---

[1] *The United Kingdom and the European Communities,* Cmnd. 4715, para. 46.
[2] Cmnd. 4715, para. 46.

the interests of the nation, does not really serve the long-term interests of private property owners (or shareholders) as a class. For even if the adverse effects of the change on the volume and quality of investment (mentioned under (1) above) are ignored, it remains true that the rate of increase of privately owned wealth will be smaller in relation to the rate of growth of national wealth than it would be under the existing system. The relation between the two (the growth of private wealth and the growth of national wealth) depends on the (consolidated) borrowing requirement of the public sector. Assuming the level of public investment and its relationship to total national investment to be given, the rate of growth of publicly owned wealth will be the greater (and the rate of growth of private wealth the smaller) the lower is the net borrowing requirment of the public sector—i.e., the higher is the level of taxation *relative to* the level of public expenditure (on both current and capital account). Hence any change which necessitates a rise in the level of taxation relative to the level of expenditure in order to preserve equilibrium will cause the rate of growth of privately owned wealth to be smaller than it would have been in the absence of that change. This also means that whilst in the short run the change will stimulate shareholders' consumption relative to the size of privately owned wealth, in the long run the standard of living of the property-owning sector of the community will not rise as much as it would have done, since in the long term it is the value of privately owned wealth which is the major determinant of the level of property owners' consumption expenditure, in comparison with which changes in the propensity to consume out of a given wealth induced by tax changes are far less important.

It may be objected that the whole of this argument assumes that the total amount of taxation raised on companies and their shareholders will be the same under the one system as under the other, whereas the true motive of the advocates of the change is to create a situation in which it becomes politically easier to reduce the burden of taxation on companies and their shareholders and politically more difficult to raise it.

But there is no real justification for any such presumption. Assuming a Conservative Government, there are no greater political obstacles to a straightforward cut of the present 40 per cent. rate of Corporation Tax to 30 per cent. than to raising that tax to 50 per cent. combined with a distribution relief of 30 per cent. Indeed the one change could be more easily justified as providing a genuine investment incentive than the other. Assuming on the other hand the return of a Labour Government which would wish to restore the burden of taxation on companies and their shareholders to a level which it considers appropriate—for example, to the equivalent of the present 40 per cent. rate of the Corporation Tax—it is true that it would find it difficult to raise the rate of tax under the new system to 61 per cent. (and still more to the 66 per cent. rate that would be required to give the equivalent yield of the 45 per cent. tax which was in force in 1970), because such high marginal rates of taxation would provide a serious disincentive to business investment. But there would be nothing to prevent a Labour Government from abolishing distribution relief in the first Budget introduced after the new administration came into power—this would be technically a very simple thing to do, whichever of the two alternative systems is adopted—and I would be surprised if the Opposition would not commit itself to do this when the proposed reform of the Corporation Tax comes to be debated in Parliament. In that event, however, shareholders might well find that they would be worse off than if the change had never been introduced; for the new Government would find it politically easier to abolish distribution relief without a corresponding reduction in the rate of the Corporation Tax than to bring about the same addition to the burden of taxation borne by shareholders through a straightforward increase in the Corporation Tax rate under the present system.

In either eventuality therefore—i.e whether the country is governed by a Conservative or by a Labour Government—there is no greater presumption of being able to protect companies and their shareholders from the "depredation" of the State, or to cause a greater alleviation in that "depredation", under the one system than under the other. Given this fact, there is a strong presumption in favour of selecting that particular system of company taxation which, at any given financial yield, secures the best results in the national interest.

Arguments in Favour of the Proposed Reform

For all the three reasons set out above the existing system of Corporation Tax is superior in my view to either of the proposed alternatives suggested in the Green Paper. It remains to examine some of the contentions that have been advanced in favour of the proposed change,[1] and this we shall now proceed to do.

(i) It has been argued that by "distributing more money to shareholders" it is possible to raise more money by way of new issues in the capital market and this will involve a more efficient allocation of national savings. But it is a fallacy to suppose that an increase in dividend payments increases the amount of money companies can raise (collectively or individually) by way of new share issues for cash. "Shareholders" do not subscribe to new issues out of the saved-up proportion of their dividend income; irrespective of their current savings out of dividends they will subscribe to new issues to the extent dictated by overall portfolio considerations. Provided new issues are made on terms that make them attractive relative to the existing range of financial investments, these will always be "taken up" by the market, through a consequential rearrangement of existing portfolios. For macroeconomic reasons which may not be immediately evident to non-economists the willingness and ability of a capital market to take up new issues is not dependent (or not to any sizeable extent) on the current level of dividend distributions.[2] And as far as individual companies are concerned, the amount of money any particular company can raise by way of rights issues (or by way of loans) is *positively* related to its rate of accumulation of reserves, and not negatively.

(ii) It has been argued that other countries (such as Germany in 1953 and France in 1965) introduced variants of the two-rate system and/or the imputation system in order to stimulate the development of a capital market and to encourage companies to raise money externally rather than by way of self-finance. This, no doubt, was the main motive behind both the German

---

[1] Cf. e.g. John Chown, *The Reform of Corporation Tax*, Institute of Fiscal Studies, 1971.
[2] I have attempted to set out the reasons for this (alas, in a mathematical form) in an Appendix to an article in the *Review of Economic Studies*, Vol. 33 (1966), pp. 316–19.

and the French reform; but there is no evidence whatever to show that the proportion of business finance raised by new issues has been significantly changed as a result. In Germany, the proportion of total financial requirements raised by new share issues for cash stubbornly remained at an insignificant 5 per cent., despite the adoption of the two-rate system with a very high rate of distribution relief. In France, the proportion is not much higher than in Germany and there is no evidence that it was significantly higher after the adoption of the new system in 1965 than it was before. In both countries the proportion of financial requirements raised by issues of ordinary shares for cash is significantly lower than in the U.K. But even in the U.K. in the period 1958–65—when the differential profits tax was no longer in existence and *before* the new Corporation Tax was introduced—no more than 8 per cent. of the total financial requirements of industrial and commercial companies was financed by issues of ordinary shares for cash; a further 22 per cent. by short- and long-term loans; and the remaining 70 per cent. out of retentions. These figures were not significantly higher than prior to 1958 when there was a two-tier profits tax with a very high non-distribution relief. Hence even with a highly developed capital market (such as the U.K. undoubtedly possesses) and a system of taxation favouring distributions and discouraging retentions, the bulk of finance for new investment comes out of ploughed back profits, and not from external sources.

(iii) It has been argued that the current U.K. system of Corporation Tax makes finance through ordinary share issues relatively more expensive than borrowing by way of debentures, mortgages or bank loans; it therefore gives an unhealthy encouragement to borrowing as a means of raising money.[1] It must of course be borne in mind that borrowing is a far more important source of external finance than ordinary share issues for cash, as is shown by the fact that in eight years prior to the introduction of Corporation Tax, three times as much money was raised by borrowing than by issues of ordinary shares. But

---

[1] Because interest on loans is a deductible expense in arriving at the chargeable profit, whereas ordinary and preference dividends are paid out of profits on which tax is charged.

apart from this, the argument that the Corporation Tax dis-
courages new issues and encourages borrowing is only valid if
the *relative yield* of shares and bonds (as measured by the price/
earnings ratio of shares and of bond yields) is taken as given.
However, precisely because the initial introduction of a Corporation Tax makes new issues relatively more expensive, it will
lead to a dearth of new issues and a consequential fall in the
yield of equities in relation to gilt-edged yields which will tend
to go on until the effect of the tax-discrimination is eliminated
and ordinary share issues are resumed. The basic reason for
this is the preference of both individual investors and financial
institutions (such as insurance companies, pension funds or
investment trusts) for keeping a certain minimum proportion
of their total assets in equities; if the normal increment of securities
outstanding takes the form of bonds rather than shares—or
rather if more new bonds are issued in relation to new shares
than the ratio in which the investing public, both institutions
and individuals, desires to hold these in their portfolios—then
equities become gradually scarcer in relation to bonds, and
equity yields will fall in relation to bond yields, so that after a
time the effect of the Corporation Tax in discouraging share
issues as against borrowing will be fully offset by the differential
cost of obtaining finance in the one form as against the other. In
other words Corporation Tax of the present type tends to generate
higher price/earnings ratios in relation to bond yields than a
Corporation Tax of the proposed type, and this rise in the price/
earnings ratios will go on until the balance between equity issues
and bond issues (ultimately governed by the preferences of
financial institutions and individual investors) is restored.
Though I know of no empirical study which has investigated this
question systematically, I believe that an inquiry of this kind
would reveal that the share of new company finance raised through
equity issues as against bond issues has not been lower in countries
which have operated the present U.K. system (such as the U.S.)
than in countries which have operated the pre-1965 U.K.
system, or the post-1953 German system. Raising money through
new ordinary issues for cash is undoubtedly easier in some countries than in others; but the main reason for this is that in some

countries company legislation provides much greater protection to the small shareholder than in other countries. In the U.K. and the U.S. the compulsory disclosure of consolidated accounts drawn up on principles defined by legislation, and the compulsory auditing of accounts by independent professional auditors, has undoubtedly contributed to a degree of public participation in the ownership of company shares which has no equivalent in the countries of the Continent of Europe. It would be wrong to suggest however that this development has been either discouraged or promoted by the nature of various systems of company taxation. The U.S. has consistently operated the same system as our present Corporation Tax whereas the U.K., before 1965, operated something akin to the proposed system (in a rather extreme form). Yet no one could say that the development in the capital market, and the spread of ownership of ordinary shares, has developed differently in the one country than the other.

(iv) Finally, it has been suggested that our present system of Corporation Tax encourages "unnecessary" retentions—i.e. the retention of profits not for purposes of the development and expansion of the business, but as a "money box"—in order to escape taxation; and as a result, complicated anti-avoidance provisions are necessary in order to prevent, or minimise, tax avoidance. The need for anti-avoidance measures in respect of close companies leading to a "great deal of complex administration" was a further "very important reason" advanced by the Chancellor in favour of the proposed change.[1]

This problem only arises in the case of "private companies" or "close companies"—i.e. companies whose ownership is concentrated in a few individuals. In the case of public companies with widespread ownership the interests of both company directors and shareholders is to limit the share of profits retained to that required for ensuring that a company's potential for expansion is not hampered by financial limitations, or by shortages of liquidity. In the case of private companies on the other hand the problem will continue to exist under the new system, even though the scope for tax avoidance will be smaller than now. Indeed,

[1] "Budget Statement", *Hansard*, 30 March 1971, col. 1384.

F

the problem existed even under the pre-1965 system and required the special anti-avoidance provision of Section 245 of the Income Tax Act, 1952.

Nevertheless it is undoubtedly true that the maximum tax that can be avoided through undue retentions will be appreciably less than under the present system—it will be surtax only, instead of both income tax and surtax. This means that assuming a top range of income tax and surtax of, say, 85 per cent. (of which 30 per cent. is income tax and 55 per cent. is the sum of surtax and the proposed "investment surcharge") for a taxpayer who is in the top range, the tax avoided through undue retentions will be 55 per cent. of income, instead of 85 per cent. as at present. Also, the number of companies whose owners are rich enough to avoid a considerable amount of tax in this way will be appreciably smaller. These are undoubted administrative advantages whose magnitude could be "quantified" in a rough way, in terms of both manpower saving by the Revenue and in terms of lower charges by accountants. I very much doubt however whether the possible savings on account of this factor could possibly be important enough to weigh against the serious economic disadvantages of the proposed system described earlier.

Relative Merits of the Two Alternatives

Assuming that the Government is determined to introduce the new system whatever its economic and social disadvantages, and assuming that it will not be prevented from doing so by the need to introduce a uniform system for the European Economic Community, there is finally the question which of the two variants—the "two-rate system" or the "imputation system"— is to be preferred.

In my view the Government is undoubtedly correct in thinking that the "two-rate system" is the more appropriate of the two, both on domestic grounds and also on international grounds, and that a return to the pre-1965 system would be the worst.

(i) The main advantage of the "two-rate system" is that it preserves the separation of company taxation and personal taxation which both the Majority and the Minority of the Royal

Commission of Taxation held highly desirable in principle.[1] This is not just a philosophical point; while the alternative "imputation system" as outlined avoids most of the inequities of the pre-1965 system (i.e., the idea of tax deemed to have been paid on a dividend whereas in fact either no tax has been received or nothing corresponding to the tax credit given) it is much more exposed to the pressure for additional concessions which would in fact gradually reproduce the same kind of ludicrous inequities which made the 1965 reform inevitable. While the "imputation system" as described in the Green Paper would ensure that the company would be liable to pay tax on at least the amount which is deemed to have been deducted on the dividend there can be little doubt that pressures would arise, sooner or later, that would undermine this principle—for example, by allowing unrelieved foreign tax against such liabilities or as a means of encouraging investment when profits are not high enough to take full advantage of capital allowances. From this point of view the "two-rate system" preferred by the Government is undoubtedly the better of the two.

(ii) From the international point of view the issue is more complex, and as van der Tempel so convincingly argued, neither is as good as our present system. However, each of the alternatives has certain international advantages over the other and the preference between them should ultimately depend on whether we regard it as more important to secure concessions through international treaties on the amount of withholding tax deducted by foreign governments on dividends paid to U.K. residents or whether we regard it as more important to be able to offer a greater tax encouragement to foreign residents investing in the U.K. Since the value of assets (in the form of direct or portfolio investment) owned by U.K. residents abroad is considerably greater than the value of the assets in the U.K. owned by foreign residents, it would appear that it is more important to have a system that gives the U.K. revenue authorities greater bargaining power in the conclusion of double taxation treaties. From this point of view the "two-rate system" which provides for a special

---

[1] Cf. Cmd. 9474, 1955, particularly paras. 56–57, also the Minority Report, paras. 95–97, reprinted in this volume.

withholding tax is a better basis for the conclusion of reciprocal arrangements than the "imputation system".

Either system would make it possible to give either greater or lesser encouragement to overseas investment in the actual provisions relating to double tax relief. The method suggested in paragraph 36 of the Green Paper would regard foreign income as marginal "and therefore most likely to be reckoned as constituting undistributed profits taxed at the 50 per cent. rate". This in my view would be highly undesirable, since it would encourage overseas investment in preference to home investment in a way that is contrary to the national interest. This will of course become a more acute problem once we enter the European Economic Community, and firms will be free to expand their productive capacity either in U.K. territory or in the rest of the Community, and to supply both the U.K. home market and other E.E.C. markets indifferently from either source. From the point of view of the level of employment and the rate of economic growth *in the U.K.* it is of course of the highest importance that the maximum encouragement be given to industrial investment in the U.K. as against investment in other industrial areas of the E.E.C. There is nothing however in either of the two proposed systems that would rule out different, and socially less undesirable, arrangements for the relief of foreign taxation than those suggested in paragraph 36 of the Green Paper.

4

TAX CREDITS: A CRITIQUE OF THE GREEN PAPER PROPOSALS[1]

THE proposals of the Green Paper contain some highly desirable features which could be considered for adoption on their own (such as the unification of income tax child allowances and family allowances); they contain other features the case for which is dubious (such as the replacement of both the single man's and the married man's allowance by tax credits, and the abandonment of a system of cumulative P.A.Y.E.) and finally features which are thoroughly obnoxious from the point of view of an equitable tax system. The case for these appears to rest on a combination of administrative considerations and the desire to throw a greater part of the burden of taxation on the lower ranges of income, while appearing to do the opposite. As will be shown below, the introduction of the tax credit scheme would in effect be a highly regressive change which, so far from helping the lower income groups would confer a net benefit on the better-off who have nothing whatever to do with social security, while the recipients of social security, taken as a group, would bear a heavier burden than under the present system, despite the fact that the proportion of the tax burden now falling on the working classes is very much greater than it was twenty or even ten years ago.

I shall consider the obnoxious aspects of the scheme first, the dubious aspects second and the desirable aspects third.

---

[1] Memorandum of Evidence submitted to the Select Committee of the House of Commons on Tax Credit. March 1973. The author wishes to acknowledge the assistance of Mr. T. F. Cripps and Mr. R. J. Tarling of the Department of Applied Economics of Cambridge University in the preparation of this memorandum.

I. THE OBNOXIOUS ASPECTS

These reside in the intention to "freeze" the income tax system into a mould which reduces it to a simple proportionate tax, levied at a uniform rate on every £ of income, irrespective of source—with the exception of the small minority of taxpayers who remain liable to surtax and/or the investment surcharge. This would mean in effect a return to the original conception of the income tax as invented by Pitt and codified by Addington which was, in the words of the Royal Commission on Taxation[1] a tax on "a body of income in gross and taxable as such however it may be distributed among its different owners". As against that a graduated income tax is necessarily a "tax on *persons* according to their respective total incomes"; it is a means of allocating the tax burden among persons so as to secure some approximation to the "equality of sacrifice" which the 1920 Royal Commission on the Income Tax recognised as the main purpose and justification of a system of progressive taxation.

On this conception income is not the object of taxation as such but merely a quantitative measure (in combination with suitable instruments for differentiating persons in different circumstances) of the taxable capacity of the individual taxpayer.

On the eve of World War II our system of income taxation in fact exhibited the features of a tax on persons according to their incomes, and the effective proportion of income paid in tax displayed a fairly smooth progression on a logarithmic scale. (See Chart I.) This was achieved in spite of the existence of a uniform standard rate up to £2,000—as a result of the high value of personal allowances (equivalent in the case of a married couple to £225 or 125 per cent. of average earnings in 1938–39) and the existence of a (fairly wide) reduced rate band, at one-third of the standard rate. In the early post-war years the *shape* of the tax curve was more or less the same, though the whole curve was pushed upwards and to the left, owing to the fact that the burden of taxation as a proportion of G.N.P. was twice as great as before

[1] Final Report. Cmd, 9474 (1955) para. 33.

the war.[1] But from 1961 onwards the smooth progression of the
tax change was gradually eroded partly by the reductions in the
number, and in the effective width, of the reduced rate bands,[2]

CHART I

Proportion of Income Paid in Tax in Various Years
(Married couples, Income All Earned)

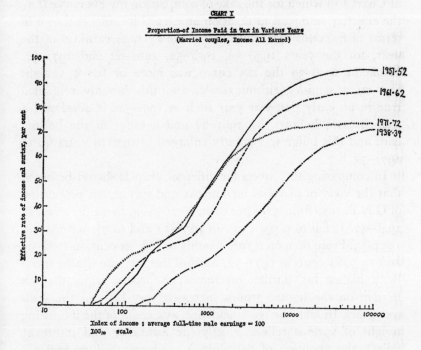

Index of income : average full-time male earnings = 100
100₁₀ scale

combined with a reduction in the standard rate from 47·5 to
38·75 per cent., and partly by the increase in the surtax limit
through personal allowances running for surtax (from 1956–57
and 1960–61 onwards) and the allowance of earned income relief

[1] This was due to the introduction of further reduced rate bands which meant
that the full standard rate became payable only at £785 or 85 per cent. *above* the
level of average earnings (which was £424).

[2] The first of such reductions occurred in Mr. Butler's Budget of 1955–56 when the
width of the first reduced band was cut from £100 to £60. The Budget of 1959–60
eliminated the third reduced band; and that of 1963–64 raised the rate on the first
band from 1s. 9d. to 4s. od. (restoring the width to £100) and the second band from
4s. 3d. to 6s. 6d. (with the width raised from £150 to £200). The widths of the reduced rate bands, totalling £300, remained thereafter unchanged until Mr. Jenkins'
second Budget in 1969–70 which eliminated the 4s. od. and left a single 6s. od. band
of £260, and his Budget of 1970–71 eliminated this last remaining reduced rate band.
Between 1952–53 and 1969–70 while average earnings rose from £450 to £1,250, a
married man's personal allowance was only raised from £210 to £375, whereas the
width of the reduced rate bands was *reduced* from £450 to £260. The significance of
these instruments of graduation was thus greatly diminished. (See also Tables 7 and
8 in the Appendix.)

and the special "earnings allowance" for surtax which raised the surtax threshold for earned income from £2,000 to over £5,000. The effects of these changes are evident from a glance at Chart I in which for the sake of comparison the tax curve (i.e., the effective rate paid in taxation on earned income) is shown in terms of fractions and multiples of the average earnings of the year, for the years 1938–39, 1951–52, 1961–62 and 1971–72. While in 1938–39 the tax curve was more or less a straight line on a semi-logarithmic scale, and this broadly remained true in an early post-war year such as 1951–52, it developed a well-shaped "hollow" by 1961–62 and a bulge at the bottom end, and this bulge was greatly enlarged in the ten years up to 1971–72.

In comparing the curves for different years it should be noted that the yield of personal income tax and surtax as a proportion of G.N.P. rose from 5·60 per cent. in 1938–39 to 12 per cent. in 1946–47. It fell to 9 per cent. in 1951–52 and to 7¾ per cent. in 1954–55. From then on it rose steadily to 10⅔ per cent. in 1964–65 and 13·5 per cent. in 1971–72. Most of this increase was financed by a higher tax burden on the wage-earners, while the tax burden on the higher groups increased very little in the post-war years. In fact, the true incidence, as a result of the increasing weight of various reliefs (chiefly life assurance and mortgage relief), the abolition of Schedule A, and greatly increased tax avoidance in the case of Schedule D income and investment income, became less heavy with the passage of years in the case of the higher income groups.

These developments made the system of income taxation progressively more inequitable in that they steadily increased the proportion of total taxation falling in the lower ranges of income. This is best shown by the figures in Table 1.[1] A married man with an income equal to the national average who paid nothing in income tax before the war, paid 8 per cent. of his income in income tax in 1951–52, 12 per cent. in 1961–62, and 19 per cent.

---

[1] In addition, Tables 7 and 8 (at the end of the Appendix) show the proportion of earnings taxed for married couples with 75 per cent. of average earnings, and with average earnings, in successive years, as well as the steady erosion of the effective tax remission given through reduced rate bands. Table 9 shows the burden of personal income tax and surtax as a proportion of GNP for those years.

in 1971–72; the burden on the man with an income of three-quarters of the national average has shown an even steeper rise from 2·5 per cent. in 1951–52 to 15 per cent. in 1971–72. As against that the man with three times average earnings or five times average earnings shows very little change in taxation over the last twenty years, and a relatively modest rise in relation to 1938–39. As Table 2 shows, the proportion of total tax receipts coming from the two-thirds of the working population with

Table 1

PERCENTAGE OF INCOME PAID IN INCOME TAX AND SURTAX

Married Couples, No Children, Income All Earned

Tax Year	Level of Incomes			
	Three-quarters of average earnings	Average earnings	Three times average earnings	Five times average earnings
	75	100	300	500
1938–39	0	0	8	14
1951–52	2·5	8	26	32
1961–62	7	12	24	26
1971–72	15	19	27	34

Note: The level of average male earnings was £180 in 1938–39, £424 in 1951–52, £787 in 1961–62, and £1,608 in 1971–72.

Table 2

CUMULATIVE DISTRIBUTION OF RECEIPTS FROM INCOME TAX AND SURTAX IN 1949–50 AND 1969–70

	Three-quarters average income	Average income	Three times average income	Five times average income	Ten times average income
1949–50	7	13	45	59	73
1969–70	9	21	76	84	92

Source: Quinquennial surveys of distribution of personal incomes.

incomes less than the national average which accounted for virtually none of the income tax receipts before the war, accounted for 13 per cent. in 1949–50 and 21 per cent. in 1969–70.[1]

[1] These figures can only be estimated for years for which quinquennial surveys of income distribution are available. The figures in Table 2 are not comparable to those in Table 1 on account of the difference in tax schedules between 1949–50 and 1951–52, and also between 1969–70 and 1971–72.

This deterioration stemmed partly from political exigencies: successive Chancellors, disinclined to raise additional revenue in the "open" way through increases in the standard rate, resorted instead to "concealed" increases brought about by letting the real value of personal allowances and of reduced bands be eroded with inflation.

But an equally important cause of these developments must be sought in the cumulative P.A.Y.E. system which required for its efficient operation that the range of income on the standard rate band should be wide and the reduced rate bands should be as few as possible (though the original justification of the system was precisely the opposite: to make it possible to operate a wide range of different marginal rates, without the need for end-year adjustments). The pressure from the Inland Revenue on successive Chancellors must undoubtedly have been in the direction of eliminating, or reducing the significance of, progression in the marginal rates of taxation for the great majority of taxpayers.[1]

These post-war developments were peculiar to Britain and were partly a heritage of the traditional system in which the "standard rate" has always played such an important role, and partly the consequence of the particular method of deduction-at-the-source adopted in the form of the cumulative P.A.Y.E. It is notable that while Britain was the first country (to my knowledge) to introduce a system of deduction-at-source for wages and salaries, none of the numerous other countries which have since adopted P.A.Y.E. have followed the British "cumulative" system. They opted instead for a much simpler system of weekly deductions which withholds from the pay of each week (or month) an amount which would be the correct deduction only if the pay of that week was the same as that of every other week in the year. (This also exists in the U.K. as a subsidiary method

---

[1] The main administrative reason for this lay in the fact that the system of cumulative P.A.Y.E. made it possible to collect the tax payable on subsidiary income not taxed at source (such as bank interest) as well as to correct for under-payment or over-payment of tax in earlier years through appropriate adjustments in the taxpayer's code number. This system operates satisfactorily so long as the taxpayer's marginal rate of taxation in the relevant range can be correctly estimated in advance. Hence the larger the proportion of taxpayers whose marginal rate of tax is liable to variation with a change in earnings, the greater the number of errors in coding and the larger the number of end-year assessments.

and is known as the "Week 1" system of deductions.) The important feature of that system is that any unevenness in the flow of income in the course of the year—whether due to extra earnings for overtime, interruption of earnings, pay rises or promotions etc.—will result in *more* tax being deducted than is due for the year, so the taxpayer has a claim for refund from the Revenue. The administrative problem resulting from such over-payments is greatly eased, in countries such as the United States, by a system of "self-assessment"—i.e., by a system which throws the responsibility for calculating the correct amount of tax payable and preparing the repayment-claim squarely on the taxpayer;[1] and since it is the taxpayer who benefits from doing this, there is a high degree of compliance.

It could be argued by the proponents of the current proposals that the proposed system is in effect no different from the system now in force and inherited from the last Labour Government, since Mr. Jenkins' last Budget had already arrived at the position in which, for the 98 per cent. of taxpayers not liable to surtax, tax was charged at a uniform rate on all chargeable income. But the difference is that whereas this has come about as a result of a series of short-term expedients adopted by successive Chancellors (egged on by their Revenue advisers) the net effect of which was a schedule of tax rates which cried out for a basic overhaul so as to restore progression, the Green Paper proposals are clearly intended to ensconce a uniform tax rate and make it a permanent and well-nigh irrevocable feature of the tax system. When every payer of income is obliged to deduct tax at source, and every claimant of relief (for mortgages, life insurance, etc.) is asked to deduct this relief at source, whatever the size or nature of the payment, it is essential to have only one rate applicable to everything—for much the same reasons for which Pitt's original system could not have embraced progression or graduation. There is a danger therefore that under the guise of introducing a system for the relief of poverty without a means test

[1] In the opinion of the Revenue, non-cumulative P.A.Y.E. with a smooth progression in the system of rates would greatly increase the administrative burden through the need for making end-year assessments for most taxpayers. Yet in the U.S. which operates such a system the Internal Revenue has only one-quarter as many employees per taxpayer as the Inland Revenue requires.

(for which it is neither necessary nor sufficient) we are asked to subscribe to the erection of a firm and lasting barrier to progressive taxation.

The one exception to this universal uniformity is the maintenance of a separate employee's contribution to social security. It is notable that while the avowed purpose of the Green Paper's proposals is "to bring together large parts of the personal taxation and social security systems" its authors have failed to take the simplest and most elementary step in that direction by merging the new employee's contributions with the payments of income tax. Since under the Government's proposals the State will only provide a flat-rate pension and not a graduated one, while the flat-rate contributions will be replaced by a levy which is proportionate to income, any pretence of the contribution being a specific payment for benefits has disappeared; and the only possible reason for maintaining a separate contribution (except perhaps for the payment of earnings related short-term benefits) is that it limits the contribution to a maximum of $1\frac{1}{2}$ times earnings (around £2,500 a year in 1972–73) and in this way succeeds in making the new system even more regressive than it would be under a single uniform rate. To charge 35 per cent. on each £ of income up to £3,000 (or more) a year and from then on charge only 30 per cent. for the next £2,500 is absurd; the more so since the employers' contribution (as distinct from the employee's) will in any case take the form of a payroll tax without consideration of individual earnings.[1,2]

The real need of the community is not to increase still further the regressive nature of our tax system, but to do the very opposite; to re-establish an equitable tax system such as Britain had in the past by restoring the same degree of progressiveness as existed before the war and in the immediate post-war decade. For that purpose it is necessary to re-introduce a progressive rate

---

[1] It is equally illogical to re-introduce the personal allowances after £5,000 a year, while denying any additional benefit on account of such allowances beyond the tax thresholds until the point of income where higher rates begin to operate. The whole conception of using tax credits for the taxpayer under £5,000 a year and tax allowances for those above makes nonsense of the "unification" of the tax system.

[2] It would be quite possible to "earmark" some proportion of receipts (say 5 per cent. of income) to the social insurance funds, without the requirement that this charge should only be levied up to $1\frac{1}{2}$ times average earnings.

schedule—not, as it was done in the past through a complex set of instruments, such as earned income relief limited to a certain maximum, reduced rate bands and surtax—but in terms of a unified schedule of rates with a surcharge on all unearned income. A schedule of marginal rates that would approximate the tax curve of 1951–52 in terms of effective rates of taxation is shown in Table 3.[1]

Table 3

1951–52 SCHEDULE OF TAX RATES; EXPRESSED IN TERMS OF A UNIFIED RATE SCHEDULE, AND IN TERMS OF 1973 "CORRESPONDING" INCOMES

Married couples without children, income all earned

Band of gross income £ p.s.					Marginal rate Per cent.
0–1,070	..	..	..	..	0
1,070–1,350	..	..	..	..	12·0
1,350–2,470	..	..	..	..	22·0
2,470–9,000	..	..	..	..	38·0
9,000–11,230	..	..	..	..	57·5
11,230–13,480	..	..	..	..	60·0
13,480–17,970	..	..	..	..	65·0
17,970–22,470	..	..	..	..	70·0
22,470–26,960	..	..	..	..	75·0
26,960–35,950	..	..	..	..	80·0
35,950–44,940	..	..	..	..	85·0
44,940–53,920	..	..	..	..	90·0
53,920–67,400	..	..	..	..	95·0
67,400	..	..	..	..	97·5

Source: See Appendix. For effective rates in 1951–52 and 1973–74 see Appendix.

In my view such a system would be much easier to operate with a non-cumulative system of deductions than with cumulative P.A.Y.E. despite the need for end-year assessments and repayments for the great majority of taxpayers. I am convinced that the cumulative system of P.A.Y.E., despite its apparent attractions, has important disadvantages, and that the Green Paper is right in claiming (paragraph 2) that the system is complicated and difficult to understand; that it lacks flexibility and requires an enormous clerical operation of re-coding every year; and that many of these disadvantages would remain even when the system is fully computerised. But the alternative need not be a

[1] The implications of 1951 rates and allowances in terms of 1972–73 values and earnings, and the changes in the distribution of incomes in the intervening years, are discussed in a separate note by T. F. Cripps and R. J. Tarling, given in the Appendix.

simple proportionate tax levied at a source at a uniform rate on all types of income, but the introduction of a system which makes end-year assessments manageable for the great majority of taxpayers, in the same way as is the case in the United States, Sweden and numerous other countries.[1] When this matter was

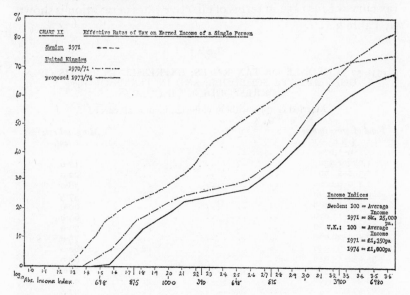

last discussed some twenty years ago the arguments against a non-cumulative system were first, that taxpayers would resent having to pay too much tax in the year and wait until after the end of the year for repayments; and second, that self-assessment is too imprecise and liable to abuse. Since then the experience gained with this system in other countries has shown that (a) over deduction and consequent annual repayments has not proved so unpopular; on the contrary, they have come to be accepted as a method of saving small amounts over the year which is then made available in a lump, normally at a time of the year when extraordinary expenses need to be incurred—e.g. before Christmas or before the summer holiday; (b) one can rely on the taxpayer to claim refunds and to operate a system of self-assessment with reasonable efficiency.

[1] A comparison of income tax charts in terms of fractions and multiples of average earnings for Sweden and the United Kingdom is shown in Chart II.

II. THE DUBIOUS FEATURES: NEGATIVE INCOME TAX

The case for some measure of integration of the income tax and social security systems on analogous lines to the Green Paper (but on a more ambitious scale) was put before the Royal Commission on Taxation by Lady Rhys Williams, the Liberal Party and Messrs. Haynes and Kirton, and after careful consideration was unanimously rejected by them.[1] Of the three main reasons given, the second and the third are relevant in the present context and are worth quoting at some length:

§52.

* * *

(2) The proposal for general cash payments without regard to means, need or circumstance seemed to us to be contrary to the generally accepted principle that, apart from family allowances, cash payments by the State should be confined to those who suffer an involuntary loss of earnings through sickness, old age or unemployment. We were not prepared to advocate a departure from this principle.

(3) For the purpose of discussing the proposals we were prepared to assume that there might be some administrative savings though those who would be most concerned with the operation of the schemes were of the opinion that it would not produce this result. We could not however escape the conclusion that any scheme which by sweeping modifications does produce significant savings would admit so little of the ordinary distinctions of equity as between one taxpayer and another as to be incompatible with our fundamental conceptions of what income tax should be.

The two important points here are first, that apart from family allowances there is no justification for paying an able-bodied man a cash supplement to his wages; this would re-introduce the "Speenhamland principle" which had such disastrous conse-

[1] *Second Report*, Cmd. 9105, April 1954, Chapter 2.

quences in the 19th century.[1] The "Beveridge principle" adopted after the last war was a different one—i.e. that entitlement to cash benefits should be confined to those who suffer a loss of earnings "through no fault of their own"—i.e. through sickness, old age and unemployment. There is nothing in the present plan that would exempt it from the traditional objections against the principle of cash supplements to wages; moreover supplementations of wages is not, as such, an important problem. Poverty in our society is mainly found among the retired, the sick, the disabled and the unemployed; low earnings are a source of poverty mainly among wage-earners with a family, and the latter could be adequately taken care of by family allowances. The residue, the man who earns too little to keep himself (and his wife, if married) is a vanishing category, particularly since most wives are earning if they don't have children to look after, and, in so far as the problem exists, calls for different remedies, such as a minimum wage.

As estimated on Table 4 below there are about three million persons without children—1·9 million single and 1·1 million married without dependants—whose annual earnings are above £420 but below the proposed thresholds (or "break-even" points) of £695 for single person and £1,040 for married persons and who would, in theory, stand to gain from the tax-credit scheme. However, an unknown proportion of them would not in fact gain (or not much) because their low annual earnings reflect the interruption of earnings during part of the year, rather than a low weekly rate of earnings throughout the year. If everybody with annual

[1] In this context it is worth quoting G. M. Trevelyan's views on the 19th century version of the negative income tax: "The enforcement of a living wage was not opposed to old English theory and practice; and it was the labourer's due in common justice, because Pitt's Acts made Trade Unions illegal. But the landlord class decided not to compel farmers to pay a living wage. They adopted instead a policy elaborated by the Berkshire magistrates at Speenhamland in 1795, namely to give rates in aid of wages . . . to prevent families from positively dying of starvation . . . It was a fatal policy for it encouraged farmers to keep down wages. But the better policy of an enforced minimum wage, though discussed, was unfortunately rejected as old-fashioned and unscientific." (G. M. Trevelyan, *History of England*, Longmans, Green 1928, pp. 583 and 612.) At the present time though trade unions are not positively made "illegal", they are prevented (as shown by the case of the hospital workers) from carrying out their normal functions of enforcing a "living wage" by the present Government's policies of statutory wage control. And I have little doubt that the authors of the Green Paper would concur in regarding the alternative policy of an "enforced minimum wage" as "old-fashioned and unscientific".

earnings below the "break-even" points were in uninterrupted employment throughout the year, the net additional payments on account of the tax credit scheme would amount to around £190 million a year. (See Table 5 on p. 158.) In fact for reasons explained below, these will only amount to some £60 million, of which only £20 million relates to single persons and married persons without children, and this £20 million is the only benefit of the scheme that could not be *equally* secured through alternative schemes for "relieving poverty" that are more effective and far less costly.

Table 4

NET TAX CREDIT ON THE GREEN PAPER PROPOSALS (SCHEDULE E TAXPAYERS; SINGLE AND MARRIED WITHOUT CHILDREN)

Lower limit	Average income	Numbers (thousands)	£m. income	Tax at 30 per cent. £m.	Credit at £208 p.a. £m.	Net Credit £m.
Single:						
420 ..	440	200·0	88·00	26·40	41·60	15·20
460 ..	475	176·6	83·88	25·16	36·73	11·57
490 ..	525	468·9	246·17	73·85	97·53	23·68
560 ..	595	510·0	303·45	91·04	106·08	15·04
630 ..	665	533·3	354·64	106·39	110·93	4·54
700 ..	—	—	—	—	—	—
Total ..		1,888·8	1,076·14	322·84	392·87	70·03

Lower limit	Average income	Numbers (thousands)	£m. income	Tax at 30 per cent. £m.	Credit at £312 p.a. £m.	Net Credit £m.
Married:						
420 ..	440	20·0	8·80	2·64	6·24	3·60
460 ..	475	21·0	9·97	2·99	6·55	3·56
490 ..	525	63·3	33·23	9·97	19·75	9·78
560 ..	595	78·1	46·47	13·94	24·37	10·43
630 ..	665	101·2	67·30	20·19	31·57	11·38
700 ..	770	259·7	199·97	59·99	81·03	21·04
840 ..	910	338·4	307·94	92·38	105·58	13·20
980 (up to £1,040)	1,010	233·2	235·53	70·66	72·76	2·10
Total ..		1,114·9	909·21	272·76	347·85	75·09
Total: Single and Married		3,300·7	1,985·35	595·60	740·72	145·12

Note: Based on 1969–70 Incomes Survey; incomes raised by 40 per cent. in each category. (Rise in earnings between 1969–70 and 1972–73 was 42·1 per cent.) Categories included are those earning £420 to £695 single and £420 to £1,040 married.

The other important point made by the Royal Commission is that simplicity cannot be reconciled with equity: whatever administrative advantages the scheme possesses cannot make up for its rigidity and for the loss of equity in the system.

These criticisms apply to a far greater degree to the Government's proposals than to the original Lady Rhys Williams' scheme which at least had the merit of making universal payments to everybody and not only to 90 per cent. of the population (who are Schedule E taxpayers). The Green Paper proposes to abolish a number of secondary allowances (the dependant allowance, the housekeeper allowance, the relief given to a single person in respect of daughter's services, and so on) on the dubious ground that under the new scheme these are no longer necessary, even though, as the Green Paper recognises, the relatives whom these allowances are intended to help "have very little income of their own" and would not be entitled under the scheme to a tax credit for themselves as they are not in regular employment (unless they are pensioners, not in receipt of supplementary benefit). This niggardliness is in sharp contrast to the care and ingenuity with which the two large anomalous reliefs in our system, the mortgage relief and the life assurance relief—both of which are ruthlessly exploited by the rich for the purpose of tax avoidance—are preserved. The abolition of these secondary allowances which are of real benefit only to people on small incomes, saves £110 million a year. The cost of mortgage and life insurance relief which is preserved intact is many times greater.

In the original Beveridge conception a comprehensive insurance scheme would have covered every citizen against all hazards from the cradle to the grave, and would have made means tested benefits unnecessary. This has not happened because enough money has never been put into the schemes to pay insurance benefits on the scale of minimum subsistence. Hence a large number of people who receive national insurance benefits need supplementation by means tested benefits. The most that can be said of the Government's scheme is that it would reduce the number of recipients on supplementary benefit but without making them any better off. It is a scheme not just of robbing Peter to pay Paul, but largely also of robbing Peter to pay Peter.

A Critique of the Present Scheme

As has been pointed out by numerous critics, the difficulty of assessing the merits of the scheme presented in the Green Paper is that it compares the existing system of taxation with an alternative scheme that "would cost about £1,300 million in relation to present circumstances" (paragraph 117). "It follows that it will only be possible to introduce the scheme at a substantial cost. But with the growth of the national income, *more resources will become available to devote to the task of eliminating poverty*: the Government consider that, taking all factors into account, and given the right order of priorities, the cost of the scheme would be a manageable one." (Paragraph 118, italics not in the original.)

However the question is not whether the resources will be "available" for sacrificing £1,300 million of revenue, now or in the future, but whether the suggested method is a sensible way of spending £1,300 million or not. There are innumerable ways of making people better off by spending money or reducing taxes and the only way any particular scheme can be judged is by examining who will benefit from it, and comparing it with some alternative scheme which costs the same amount. It will be shown that it would be possible to "eliminate poverty" far more effectively at half the cost of the present scheme—which is not difficult because, as we shall show, *none* of the net cost of the £1,300 million is spent on the poor.

The Government has managed to convey a wholly misleading impression of the implications of their proposals by two devices. First, by comparing two alternative systems of taxation, one of which yields £1,300 less than another, instead of comparing them in terms in which the two alternatives have the same yield;[1] secondly, by showing in all the illustrative examples the net benefit accruing from the scheme at different levels of income in terms of *weekly* earnings, and thereby concealing the fact that the scheme has very different implications (for the great majority

[1] It will be shown below that on an "equivalent revenue basis"—i.e. by assuming that the same net benefits are given in the form of tax credits as in the Green Paper, but in annual and not only in weekly terms, the scheme would cost £1,530m. and require an increase in the basic rate of income tax to 40 per cent. if the same "thresholds" are to be maintained.

of people who are shown to benefit from the payment of tax credits) in terms of *annual* earnings.

The scheme can be "decomposed" into the following main features:

(i) An increase in income tax personal allowances for all those single persons and married persons who are above the taxpaying threshold. "Tax credits" of £4 a week (£208 a year) for a single person, £6 a week (£312 a year) for the married person are the equivalent in terms of income tax allowances to £695 and £1,040 respectively, which means that the single person's allowance is raised by £100 and the married person's by £265, equivalent to a tax reduction of £30 for every income-tax payer who is single and £79·50 for the married. (Since these new allowances also qualify for surtax, the maximum tax benefit for the top-range surtax payer on earned income is £75 for the single man and £208 for the married man.)

(ii) The payment of "negative income tax" (or net tax credit) to all regular Schedule E taxpayers (i.e., people in regular employment) whose incomes are *below* the tax thresholds indicated above;

(iii) The taxation of all social security cash benefits not now taxable—i.e., unemployment and sickness insurance, maternity allowance and invalidity pension would become taxable;

(iv) Income tax child allowances and family allowances would be abolished and replaced by a tax credit of £2 a week for each child, regardless of age. For a taxpayer whose income is high enough to take full benefit from the child allowances and does not benefit from that part of family allowances which is subject to claw-back, this is equivalent to a net tax remission (for a child under 11) of £44 a year for the first child, £29·50 for the second child and £25·50 for third and subsequent children.

(v) The replacement of supplementary benefit payments by tax credits for about two million pensioners and for many of the insurance beneficiaries who draw supplementary benefits during periods of sickness or unemployment.

Table 5 shows the estimated effect of these changes, separating out the relief given to taxpayers on account of the rise in personal allowances and the amounts paid in negative income tax (or net tax credits) to those whose incomes are below the "thresholds" where negative tax comes into operation.

It has also been possible to show the distribution of the benefits from the whole scheme for people with incomes below and above £1,000 a year.[1] Apart from over 3 million pensioners there are nearly 2 million single persons and around 1 million married couples in the category, and the latter includes 450,000 families with around 1 million children.

The amazing feature of these tables is that the cost of the scheme is not due to the payment of negative income tax at all, since the tax credits, totalling £850 million will be more than recouped by savings of £1,040 million resulting from the reduction in social security payments of various kinds and the withdrawal of minor allowances.[2] The rise in personal allowances which will only benefit people with incomes above the *present* tax-paying thresholds will amount to £1,470 million, or £170 million more than the total cost of the scheme; and of this sum (as shown by Table 6) no less than £1,394 million will accrue to people with incomes over £1,000 a year. The net benefit to everyone *under* £1,000 a year (including pensioners) is only £150 million and this is more than offset by the losses in social security benefits of people with incomes *over* £1,000.

The explanation is that any single person with an *annual* income above the *present* tax thresholds is made worse off by the scheme if he has an interruption of earnings (on account of sickness and unemployment) for more than 15 weeks of the year; this means every single person working 37 weeks or less in the

---

[1] The necessary information was mainly derived from answers to two Parliamentary questions, given on 24th January and 12th February.

[2] This does not comprise the savings due to the abolition of age exemption relief (which were deducted from the increased cost of the allowances). For reasons explained below, the savings in supplementary benefits could also be £80 million greater than the £250 million shown in Table 5, if the "F.A.M." definition of children was substituted for the "Schedule E" definition.

Table 5

COST OF TAX CREDIT SYSTEM

		£m.	£m.
(1)	Value of increased single and married allowances[1] ..	1,020	
(2)	Value of increased child allowances[2]	450	
	Net increase in Tax Allowances		1,470
(3)	*Negative tax* (excess of tax credits over tax paid) to those below the net thresholds paid to:		
	Schedule E Taxpayers[3]..	190	
	Pensioners[4]	280	
	Children	380	
	Total Tax Credits		850
	Total Cost		2,320
(4)	*Less Savings* on account of:		
	Tax on short-term benefits of those *above* new threshold	150	
	Tax on short-term benefits of those *below* threshold..	80	
	Saving in Supplementary Benefit[5]	250	
	Saving in F.A.M., F.I.S., N.I. Benefits for children[6]	430	
	Other savings (minor allowances, etc.)	110	
	Total Savings		−1,020
	Net Cost		1,300

[1] This is the net cost of raising the single man's allowance by £100 and the married man's allowance by £265 and leaving the wife's earned income relief unchanged. If the latter were raised in the same way as the single man's allowance the cost would be £230m. higher. It is net of saving in age exemption relief.

[2] This is made up of the following items:

	£m.	£m.
Increased cost of raising child allowances from the present average of £230 a year to £347 (assuming the present level of single and married allowances)	+450	
Saving due to reduced absorption of allowances due to the rise in the single and married allowances	−200	
Remission of present taxes on F.A.M. and claw-back on F.A.M.	+200	
Total		450

[3] Derived from Table 4. See note [1] to Table 6 opposite.

[4] Derived from *Hansard*, 24th January 1973, col. 188.

[5] This is made up as follows:

	£m.	£m.
Pensioners	200	
Short term N.I. beneficiaries..	40	
Children	10	
Total		250

[6] This is made up as follows:

	£m.	£m.
F.A.M.	350	
N.I. Benefits for children	70	
F.I.S.	10	
Total		430

Table 6

NET BENEFITS AND COSTS OF THE TAX CREDIT SYSTEM FOR
THOSE WITH INCOMES BELOW AND ABOVE £1,000 A YEAR

£m.

Item	Below £1,000	Above £1,000	Total
A. ADULTS			
(1) Increase in tax-free allowances for single and married persons	+90	+930	+1,020
(2) Payments of Tax Credits:			
(a) To Schedule E taxpayers (gross)	+190[1]	—	+190
(b) To Pensioners (net)	+80[2][3]	—	+80
(3) *Saving* through the taxation of insurance benefits, supplementary benefits, etc.	−220[4]	−160	−380[5]
Net Cost ..	+140[3]	+770	+910
B. CHILDREN			
(4) Increase in income tax allowances ..	−16[6]	+466	+450
(5) Cost of tax credits *net* of savings in F.A.M., F.I.S., N.I. and Supplementary Benefits	+10[3] +26	+380 −86[8]	+390 −60[7]
Total	+150[3]	+1,150[9]	+1,300

[1] This is the *gross* amount paid throughout the year to recipients other than pensioners. It is derived from the estimate in Table 4 (rounded to the nearest £10m.) plus an allowance of £40m. for the additional benefit of the tax credit scheme (imputable to the married allowance) to married persons with children. The net amount (after deduction of savings in insurance benefits etc.) comes to −£30m., or to +£60m. including the £90m. benefit resulting from the increase in single and married allowances. Of this £60m. only £20m. relates to single and married persons without children. (See *Hansard*, January 24th 1973, Written Answers, col. 188.)

[2] This is the *net* amount paid out after deducting the saving of supplementary benefits; it relates to the one-third (or 1 million) pensioners who fail to claim their present entitlement to supplementary benefits.

[3] Source: *Hansard*, 24th January 1973, col. 188.

[4] Derived by difference from the figures given in *Hansard, op. cit.* and the sum of items (1) and (2a) above.

[5] This is composed of the following items: £m.
Savings in National Insurance Benefits 230
Net Savings in Supplementary Benefits of Insured Persons other than Pensioners 40
Savings through the abolition of minor allowances, etc. 110

380

[6] Loss due to inability to absorb existing child allowance.

[7] This is the difference between £380 million cost of the tax credits given to children, £380 million shown in line 3 of Table 5 and £430 million in line 4 of Table 5 plus £10 million on account of supplementary benefits.

[8] Derived by difference from the +£26 million shown in col. 1 and the −£60 million in col. 3.

[9] According to the table given in *Hansard*, 12th February 1973, Written Answers col. 271–72, of the £1,150 million, £400 million benefits taxpayers with incomes of less than £1,600 a year, £500 million those of £1,600–£2,500, £200 million those of £2,500–£5,000 and £50 million those above £5,000.

year who earns more than £16·40 per week. Similarly every married person working 27 weeks or less and earning more than £28·60 a week (when working) will be worse off. This is because for people who are at or above the present tax-paying limits in annual terms, the benefit of the higher tax allowances inherent in the scheme are offset by the taxation of their national insurance benefits, provided they draw such benefits for more than 15 weeks in the year in the case of a single person and more than 25 weeks in a year in the case of a married person.[1]

For illustration let us take the case of a single man who earns £30 a week, works for 26 weeks and draws unemployment pay for the rest of the year. Under the present system, he pays the cumulative sum of £152·78 in tax under P.A.Y.E., all but £55·50 of which is refunded to him in the second half of the year during which he also received a weekly tax-free insurance benefit of $26 \times £6·75 = £175·50$. Hence his annual post-tax receipts are $780 - 55·50 + 175·50 = £900·00$. Under the new system he pays tax at 30 per cent. on $£780 = £234$, and receives credit of $26 \times 4 = £104$ in the first half of the year, a net income of $£780 - 130 = £650$. In the second half of the year he pays tax of 30 per cent. on £175·50, or £52·50 which is more than balanced by tax credits of £104, making a net receipt of $-175·50 + 52·5010 = 4 = 227·00$. His annual receipt is therefore £877 or £23 *less* than it is at present; his extra receipts due to "negative income tax" in the second half of the year is more than balanced by the heavier taxation of his earnings in the first half.

There is of course a re-distribution of income involved in the scheme but it is carefully designed to ensure that it is *within* the same social classes—it is paid by the (longer term) sick and unemployed to the net benefit of those who are poor for other reasons.[2] The benefit goes to people (estimated about a million) who do not claim supplementary allowances for which they are

---

[1] The single person's tax threshold is raised by £100 (worth £30 in tax) and the married person by £265 (worth £79·50 in tax). Hence the 30 per cent. tax on insurance benefits balances the gain when the total of such benefits received exceeds £100 in the year for the single man ($15 \times £6·75$); or £265 in the year for the married man ($25 \times £10·90$).

[2] Apart from pensioners, the true net beneficiaries are low paid workers employed throughout the year: at the figures suggested in the Green Paper, these would be mostly young girls in the service industries: assuming that their employers really *pay* the tax credit and do not pocket the money by paying lower nominal wages.

eligible and who will receive tax credits automatically; the credit, averaging £2 per week will bring them towards, but not quite up to, the supplementary allowance level. Another three million people whose incomes (including sickness or unemployment pay) are above the supplementary allowance level but below the new tax thresholds will gain because the tax credit scheme ensures that they will receive the full tax-equivalent of the personal allowances instead of only that part by which their income exceeds the old tax thresholds. It should be noted that people who at present claim supplementary allowances and other means tested benefits stand to gain little or nothing other than being relieved of the bother of having to make out a claim for the benefits.

But these gains, as we have seen, are more than balanced by the losses of those whose incomes are at or above the *new* thresholds in annual terms, but who receive insurance benefits for more than a certain fraction of the year. The losses of the latter group exceed the gains of the former by about £100 million.

There would be nothing wrong in principle with taxing unemployment and sickness benefits, providing that on the first introduction of the scheme the nominal value of the benefits was raised so as to ensure that the *net* value of benefits after tax was maintained for people in lower income groups. This could be done, in the framework of the present scheme, by increasing the nominal value of the (pre-tax) benefits by 44 per cent. at an additional cost of around £250 million. But if this were done, the question of *why* it is necessary to give away as part of the operation of eliminating poverty £1,150 million to people with incomes of £1,000 a year or over (of which £850 million goes to taxpayers with over £1,600 a year) becomes even more pertinent.

A far more attractive scheme than the negative income tax is the "new Beveridge plan" put before the 1970 meeting of the British Association in Durham by Professor Atkinson.[1] According

---

(This would be easier to do for small employers than under the old Speenhamland system, since the supplementation of wages is not administered through local authorities or the D.H.S.S., but is left to the employer himself.)

[1] A. B. Atkinson, Conflict in Social Security Policy, in *Conflicts in Policy Objectives*, Basil Blackwell, Oxford, 1971, pp. 20–37.

to this plan both national insurance benefits and family allowances would be raised to the supplementary benefit scale; the excess over current levels being subject to a "claw-back" (such as the "claw-back" introduced in 1968 in connection with the increase in family allowances). In this way everyone except a small minority of low-wage employees would be given an automatic entitlement to income sufficient to lift them to the accepted minimum subsistence levels; and the claw-back would ensure that the cost would not be prohibitive. The cost, originally estimated at £525 million, would not amount to more than £700 million or only a little more than one-half of the Green Paper scheme; but with the important difference that *all* the money would genuinely go to the relief of poverty instead of a negative amount, as under the Government's scheme.

The operation of a "claw-back" requires however that for the main family earner at least, the system of a tax-free personal allowance be retained and not be replaced by "tax-credits". The claw-back operates by *withdrawing* the benefit in whole or in part from those who are above a certain income level; and under our system this can most conveniently be done by a reduction in the tax-free allowance through an appropriate change in the taxpayer's code number.[1] Another form of "claw-back" would be to tax insurance benefits at a higher rate—say at 45 per cent. instead of 30 per cent., above the tax-paying limits (which are higher for people in retirement). For these reasons alone (as well as the avoidance of large uncovenanted benefits to the well-to-do, as under the Government's scheme) there is a strong case for the retention of the main personal allowances, i.e. the single person's and the married man's allowance, as well as the married woman's earned income relief.

There may however be a case for giving the *same* allowance to an earner whether he is single or married, and to withdraw any additional relief for marriage except for those (*a*) who have children; (*b*) who are above working age. In the case of a married woman with children, the additional allowance could be given as

---

[1] Under the P.A.Y.E. system this would require subsequent adjustment (in the year or years following) for any irregular short-term benefit on account of sickness or unemployment which could not be "coded in" beforehand.

an additional credit to the family allowances, administered
through vouchers payable at the Post Office when they are not at
work; if the wife takes up employment, the book of vouchers
would have to be surrendered to the employer, who would
then operate P.A.Y.E. by giving the single person's tax-free
allowance on her earnings (in place of the wife's credit) and the
children's tax credits (according to the vouchers) as part of her
weekly pay. This would mean that in the case of women under
60, either the "mother's credit" of say, £2 a week, or a single
person's earned allowance could be claimed, but not both. With
this system it would be reasonable to put the single person's earned
income allowance at somewhere mid-way between the present
single person's allowance and the married allowance (say at £700
a year, with a two-sevenths reduction in the case of investment
income) which would make the joint allowance of husband and
wife £1,400 a year in the case where both are earning; or the
equivalent of £700 + £350 = £1,050 in the case where the wife
is not earning but has children with regard to whom she is in
receipt of a family allowance, or else is over pensionable age;
but it would restrict the allowance to £700 a year in the case of
such married couples who are of working age but have no children
to support, and where the wife is not earning and is not incapacitated.[1]

This scheme would deal with all cases of poverty except those
which are due to such a low rate of earnings that they do not
provide a minimum livelihood for the single person even when in
continual employment. That this is not in itself an important
category is shown by the fact that only about £20 million of the
Government's £1,300 million scheme for "eliminating poverty"
would go to relieve poverty in cases of this kind. And the best
way to deal with this category of cases is to introduce a legal
minimum wage (or otherwise ensure that no one employs a
man on a full-time basis on a wage that is below minimum subsistence) and not by negative income tax.

A negative income tax is a very wasteful method of relieving

[1] The latter category comprises less than one-quarter of the number of married
women with respect to whom married allowance is given. (See *Hansard*, 24th January
1973, Written Answers, cols. 189–190.)

poverty; if it is applied on a scale sufficient to make any substantial difference at or near the poverty level, the increase
in taxation required to finance it is very much greater than the
cost of securing comparable relief by other methods. It is no
accident that the Government presented a scheme which benefits
the well-to-do and the rich at the expense of the poor, and did
not say how it would be financed. If we add to the £1,300 million
net cost of the Green Paper scheme the £230 million needed to
maintain the present value of (short-term) national insurance
benefits, we need an addition of no less than 25 per cent. in the
basic rate of income tax (i.e. from 30 per cent. to 37·5 per cent.)
to get the required revenue from those above the tax-paying
thresholds. But this in turn requires that the tax-credits be raised
by 25 per cent. in order to preserve the same tax-thresholds and
to give an equivalent benefit by way of negative income tax.
This makes a further addition to the cost which in turn requires
that the basic rate of tax be increased further, until by a series of
diminishing steps, a state of balance is attained. Thus to finance
the scheme by increases in the basic rate without reducing the
real value of tax credits, requires a 33⅓ per cent. increase in both
the basic rate of tax and in the tax credits: i.e. a basic rate of
40 per cent. and tax credits of £8 a week instead of £6 (for the
married man). With the rate increased from 30 to 40 per cent.
single persons will still be better off if their incomes are up to
£300 higher than the new threshold (that is, up to an income of
£995), and married couples will be better off if their incomes
are up to £800 higher, in other words up to an income of £1,840
a year.[1,2]

[1] Under the Government's scheme, with every £ of income taxed, each 1 point
addition to the basic rate adds £400 million to the revenue. The *gross receipt* from a
10 point addition in income tax is therefore £3,600 million. However in order to
preserve the same break-even points as shown in the tables in the Green Paper the
tax credits would also have to be raised by 33⅓ per cent. which in turn would add
£2,475 million to the gross outlay on tax credits, leaving less than enough to cover
the net outlay of £1,530 million. It would thus require raising and repaying staggering
sums to effect a relatively modest re-distribution of income in favour of the poor.

[2] On the other hand if the present tax thresholds were kept unchanged and not
raised—which would mean paying £3·43, £4·47 and £1·33 a week in tax credits to
the single man, the married man and the child, respectively, instead of the figures
used in the Green Paper—the introduction of the scheme, so far from costing anything, would bring a net gain of £580m. to the Exchequer. For the tax credits of
£850m. shown in Table 5 would be reduced to £340m. whereas the savings in benefit
payments and allowances would only fall from £1,020m. to £920m.

The conclusion is inescapable that in practice it will not prove possible to give any *worthwhile benefit* in the form of universal tax credits to those who need it without giving a much larger uncovenanted benefit to those who do not need it. This in itself constitutes a strong argument for rejecting the scheme.

But there are other, equally strong arguments. If we are to restore an equitable and a truly progressive system of taxation it is essential that the vast concessions now given in the form of mortgage relief and life insurance relief be gradually liquidated. Since the sudden withdrawal of these concessions would create hardship for many owner occupiers in the lower ranges of income the withdrawal must be gradual. The first step must be to set limits to the total amounts that any taxpayer can claim for either mortgage relief or life insurance relief (as well as interest on personal loans). Second, a minimum tax-free allowance should be introduced, comprising both personal allowances and other reliefs, and it is this minimum allowance which should be raised in future to offset the "fiscal drag", rather than the personal allowance as such. In this way, over a period of years, the value of mortgage and life assurance reliefs could be phased out without the taxpayer at any time having his post-tax income reduced. This would also reduce substantially the cost of increasing the allowances.

Such reforms would be ruled out if the Green Paper's scheme was adopted which offers what is in effect a flat-rate subsidy on all such payments, the largest benefit of which would accrue to taxpayers in the higher ranges of income.

In judging the likely level of allowances at the time of their introduction (in real terms) account must also be taken of the fact that the present fiscal system is not a viable one, in that the Government has cut taxation in the last two years by £3,000m. without any corresponding reduction in the scale of public expenditure. Assuming that last year's increase in income tax allowances costing £1,200m. will have to be "clawed back" through higher rates of taxation sooner or later, the required basic rate of income tax—for the payments of tax credit on the scale of the Green Paper in real terms—would be more like 50 per cent. than 40 per cent. Apart from its disincentive effects, a basic rate of tax of that order is bound to be highly inflationary in its effects on wage claims, since it would require an addition of £4 to the gross pay to compensate a worker for a rise in living costs by £2.

III. THE DESIRABLE FEATURES: A UNIFIED SYSTEM OF FAMILY ENDOWMENT

While there is no case for scrapping our existing tax system for the sake of introducing universal tax credits for everybody, there is a strong case (in my view) for a unification of the present income tax child allowances and family allowances. This has been in force in Sweden for the past 25 years and more recently has been introduced in Denmark. (It may also have been adopted in other countries.) Neither of these countries introduced a universal system of negative income tax.

The advantages of this reform need little elaboration. Our present system of helping the family through a multiplicity of instruments—income tax child allowances, F.A.M. without claw-back, F.A.M. with claw-back, and finally F.I.S.—is the product of a haphazard development, unnecessarily complicated and also costly in relation to its effectiveness.[1]

The Green Paper's proposals, though they leave the question open whether the children's credit should be paid to the father or the mother, have a number of objectionable features:

   (i) They confine the credit to children whose parent or parents are regular Schedule E taxpayers, thus leaving an unknown proportion of children outside its scope, including those of the 300,000 unmarried or divorced etc. mothers in need of supplementary benefit. The present family allowances are universal, and it would be a retrograde step to confine the future allowances to the children of Schedule E parents only.

  (ii) The Green Paper proposes a uniform credit of £2 a week per child, irrespective of age, whereas in terms of "value for money" it would be far better to vary the credits (or allowances) according to age, as is the case with supplementary benefits.

 (iii) The allowances, being in the nature of a "tax credit" are not subject to tax, whereas the present family allow-

---

[1] F.I.S. is very "cheap" but this is partly because the majority entitled to it do not make use of it.

ances are, and the Green Paper proposes that other social security benefits, not now subject to tax, should be taxed. If the allowances were taxable, the amount of help that could be given to the poor, for any given total of expenditure, would be much greater.

There is a strong case therefore for segregating the proposals relating to the unification of income tax child allowances and family allowances from the rest of the Green Paper's proposals; and since child poverty is a serious and deplorable feature of our society there are strong grounds for introducing a unified system of family endowment as soon as possible.

There are important advantages in retaining the present system of payment through vouchers issued by the Ministry of Social Security encashable by the mother at the Post Office. Apart from the fact that there is no other convenient way of paying these allowances to mothers who are not in regular employment, an age-graduated credit would be too complicated to administer on the lines of the Green Paper.

A further advantage of this scheme is that paying *all* children £2 a week through the Post Office tax-free (and abolishing income tax child allowances) would cost £350 million only,[1] whereas the net cost of paying the *same* tax credits to Schedule E children only (as shown in Table 6) comes to £390 million. The explanation for this apparent paradox is twofold. First, the extension of tax-credit on a F.A.M. basis to 300,000 non-Schedule E mothers would be virtually costless: since all such mothers now draw supplementary benefits. Second, the Green Paper scheme reckons the cost on an income-tax allowance basis, which means giving credit to non-resident children and to students over 18 who are not eligible for F.A.M. Thus while the total number of children (around 15 milllion) happens to be the same in the two cases, they are not all the same children; and paying the income-tax children (university students or children abroad) is far more costly, precisely because they are not in need and do not draw supplementary benefits.

There is also a clear case for making these allowances the same

[1] See *Hansard*, 24th January 1973, col. 190.

as those applicable to supplementary benefits, which at current levels are £1·90 for children under 5, £2·25 for 5–10, £2·75 for 11–12, £3·40 for 13–15, £4·05 for 16–17 and £5·20 for 18–20. The weighted average of these rates (allowing for the proportion of children in the higher age groups who are not in full-time education) comes to £2·56 per child per week, which would mean an additional cost of £760 million compared with the net cost of the present income tax child allowances and family allowances, and £410 million more than the £350 million costs of giving a tax-free allowance of £2 to each child irrespective of age.

If these family allowances were made taxable in the same way as other social security benefits, the net cost of paying age-related family allowances for each child on the above scale would be reduced from £760 million to around £200 million. However it would be administratively more convenient to have a simple claw-back scheme whereby the main family earner's tax-free allowance is abated by, say, £100 a year with respect to each child (irrespective of age) in receipt of family allowances for a full year. This would "claw-back" £30 a year, or 56p a week from each child, and reduce the net cost of the scheme from £760 million to £310 million.[1]

A mother's credit of £2 per week on the lines suggested above could be paid, alongside the family allowances, to mothers who have children and do not take a job owing to their family responsibilities. This credit would not be available to mothers whose Schedule E income exceeds the single person's tax-free allowance; to ensure this, mothers on taking up regular employment would have to hand over their book of vouchers to the employers who would then pay the family allowances as an addition to the weekly net pay (net after tax) and return the vouchers to the Inland Revenue along with the cheques sent in connection with P.A.Y.E. collections. This would end the anomalous situation by which in the case of a married couple both earning, both draw a single person's allowance and the husband

---

[1] This scheme would still leave the family above the present tax threshold appreciably better off than under the present combined system of income tax allowances and F.A.M. But any higher taxation of family allowances would only be feasible under some scheme which deducts tax from the allowances paid directly, and not by way of abatement of tax-free allowances on the husband's (or wife's) earnings, which may give rise to complicated administrative problems.

gets a wife's allowance as well, whether or not they have dependent children.[1] It would save around £125 million in revenue, in
relation to the present system.[2]

In relation to the Green Paper scheme the saving would be very
much greater: of the order of £500 million. This is because the
Green Paper scheme nearly doubles the present differential
between the single person's allowance and the married allowance,
only a small part of which is "clawed back" through the restriction on the wife's earned income relief. By increasing the
additional allowance on account of marriage from £180 to
£345, the cost to the Exchequer is raised from £625 million to
£1,200 million, while the restriction on the wife's earned income
relief saves £230 million only. This is a wholly unjustified outlay,
more appropriate to a scheme for subsidising idle wives than to a
scheme for eliminating poverty.

The Green Paper does not explain why this greatly increased
differential is justified or necessary. It refers however to the
recommendations of the Royal Commission on Taxation[3]
which held in 1954 that the differential in favour of the married
woman was too great if she gets a full personal allowance while
her husband draws a married allowance as well, and it said, in
paragraph 134:

> The most natural course would be to withhold the net
> marriage allowance of the husband in accordance with some
> scheme that reduced its value progressively in proportion to
> the size of the wife's tax-free earnings. But enquiry satisfied
> us that any such scheme for a graduated reduction of the
> marriage allowance is ruled out owing to its administrative
> complications.

It then went on to recommend a reduction of the wife's earned
income relief, but only if its other recommendation concerning a
minimum earned income relief were adopted.

---

[1] The married allowance would continue to be paid to the husband when either
party, or both, reach the normal age of retirement or when the wife is incapacitated.
[2] The gross savings from the abolition of married allowances would come to £625
million. Paying a mother's credit to all mothers not at present in employment with
an income of more than £595 a year would cost £500 million.
[3] *Second Report*, Cmd. 9105.

G

The Royal Commission on Taxation's view was therefore rather a different one from the impression given in the Green Paper, and that was twenty years ago. Since then social conditions have radically changed and there are few women today who would prefer not to have a job if they have no children—almost irrespective of the economic circumstances of their husbands. I am quite sure therefore that if the question were examined afresh by a similar body today their recommendation would be to restrict the married allowance on the lines indicated above, and not the wife's earned income relief.

There may be something to be said for retaining the income tax child allowance for the oldest child for a transitional period (or paying its equivalent by way of tax credit to the main earner) both to enable the Ministry of Social Security to cope with the problem of extending the system of family allowances to first children, and to moderate the tax-effect of transferring the benefit of children's allowances from the father to the mother, which would be the more severe if it were combined with the withdrawal of the married allowance—even though, as a more permanent arrangement, a compromise of this kind would not have much to be said for it in logic.

IV. CONCLUSIONS

(1) The tax credit scheme in the Green Paper has only administrative simplicity to recommend it in a field in which, in the unanimous judgment of the Royal Commission on Taxation, administrative simplicity can only be bought at a cost in equity which would be "incompatible with our fundamental conceptions of what income tax should be". Apart from the families which could be equally helped through a revised system of family allowances, it would be of net benefit only to a relatively small group of men and women who have low weekly earnings uninterrupted throughout the year by sickness or unemployment. This is achieved at an enormous cost in lost revenue, all of which goes to the benefit of taxpayers with incomes above the tax-paying thresholds; the people who are supposed to benefit from the payment of tax credits are in fact made around £100 million

worse off as a result of the scheme. If the terms of the scheme were so revised as to make the scheme self-balancing in revenue terms, the necessary additional taxation to be raised (to give the same net benefits in the form of net tax credit in the lower ranges of income, and in terms of annual and not just weekly earnings) would require an increase in the basic rate of income tax from 30 to 40 per cent. The same relief to poverty could be secured at a fraction of this cost by alternative methods.

(2) There are objections in principle to paying a supplement to wages to able-bodied persons in employment, which are mitigated but not removed by the circumstances (*a*) that the supplement is only paid to persons who are in regular employment, and not to the work-shy; (*b*) that the net supplementation of wages is too small to be of any great consequence.

(3) The administrative advantages of the scheme depend on the abolition of graduation for the 98 per cent. of taxpayers not liable to surtax; and the curtailment of differentiation through the abolition of a number of secondary allowances most of which benefit the poorer sections of the community while leaving intact existing concessions of an anomalous nature which mostly benefit the rich.

(4) There is a case for unifying the existing income tax child allowances and family allowances in a system of tax-free age-graduated family allowances payable to the mother. It may be expedient to pay the father the allowance with respect to the first child for a transitional period. These allowances should be paid on supplementary benefit scales. There is a case for applying a simple system of claw-back so as to withdraw the extra benefit from people whose incomes are above the tax thresholds, thereby keeping down the cost to a level which makes the introduction of the scheme feasible.

(5) There is equally a case for raising both short-term social security benefits (unemployment and sickness benefits) and pensions to the supplementary benefit scale, making them taxable at the same time. In the case of pensions, it would be appropriate to operate a "claw-back" system through the treatment of pensions as unearned income, liable to tax above the age-exemption limit at the rate applicable to investment incomes.

(6) There is also a case for substituting a "mother's credit" of £2 a week for the existing wife's allowance (i.e. the difference between the married allowance and the single allowance) in the case of married couples of working age where the wife is not incapacitated. This would remove the present anomaly by which a married couple of working age is entitled to two single person's allowances and also the wife's allowances; the mother's credit being set off against the wife's earned income allowance when in employment.

(7) It is a major defect of the Government's scheme and of the present system of direct taxation in the United Kindgom that alone amongst the tax systems of advanced countries it applies a single rate of tax to the taxed income of 98 per cent. of taxpayers, instead of having, as was the case up to 1969–70, a system of graduated rates at the bottom of the scale as well as at the top. The adoption of the Government's scheme would effectively prevent a return to graduation for taxpayers at the lower end of the income scale. Social justice requires a change in the opposite direction. This could be achieved by re-introducing reduced rate bands and by applying rates higher than the present basic rate at a lower starting point. (A first band of £250 charged at 15 per cent., a second band of £250 charged at 25 per cent, and a third band of £250 at 30 per cent. could be made self-balancing by a rise in the rates of tax for incomes in excess of £1,500 by 10 points.[1]

(8) It is a matter for examination whether the system of cumulative P.A.Y.E. should be retained or replaced by a simpler system of non-cumulative weekly deductions (as exists in other countries) irrespective of whether the tax-credit scheme and/or the system of uniform tax rates is adopted or not.

---

[1] This would reduce the burden by a maximum of £50 on incomes £1,375–£1,625 (in the case of married couples) and provide some relief up to £2,025.

APPENDIX

THE 1951–52 INCOME AND SURTAX SYSTEM APPLIED TO 1973

(By T. F. Cripps and R. J. Tarling)

One indication of the increase in average pre-tax income between 1951 and 1973 is the increase in average full-time male earnings. This is expected to have risen from £424 to £1,900—a ratio of 4:48. An alternative method is to estimate the change in the number of actual and potential taxpayers (the latter defined as the number exempt on grounds of low income) and compare this with the increase in total personal income before tax. The number of potential and actual taxpayers may be approximated by the number of males and single females aged 18 and over; this has risen by $5\frac{1}{4}$ per cent. from 24,712 thousand in 1951 to 26,009 thousand in 1973. Total personal income will have increased from £11,948 million in 1951 to about £56,500 million in 1973, implying that average income per taxpayer (actual or potential) has risen from £483 to £2,173—a ratio of 4:49. This confirms the evidence of the change in average male earnings.

Now if

(a) the 1951–52 tax thresholds and bands are multiplied by this ratio;

(b) the 1951–52 rules and tax rates are otherwise maintained unchanged;

(c) the distribution of taxpayers across taxable categories (i.e. income distribution) is unchanged;

and

(d) the ratio of total personal income before tax to G.D.P. remains the same as in 1951–52;

then the yield of income and surtax should be in the same ratio to G.D.P. as in 1951–52.

In fact the ratio of total personal income to G.D.P. will have risen from 94·6 per cent. in 1951 to about 98·0 per cent. in 1973. The yield, expressed as a proportion of G.D.P. should therefore be higher than in 1951–52 unless income distribution has become considerably more progressive in the relevant sense. Part of the increase in the ratio of total personal income to G.D.P. is accounted for by increased grants some of which are not taxable. But after deducting *all* current grants from the public sector from total personal income, the ratio has not fallen significantly.

It is difficult to obtain good estimates of changes in the distribution of personal income before tax. Using the quinquennial surveys combined with demographic estimates of the total of actual and potential taxpayers, it is possible to obtain a rough comparison of cumulative distributions of income before tax in 1949–50 and 1969–70. To make the income scale comparable, the bands in 1949–50 are multiplied by an estimate of the ratio of average pre-tax income per taxpayer (actual or potential) in 1969 to that in 1949.

Upper limit of income range (1969 income equivalents)	Cumulative proportions 1949	1969
330		16·4
400		19·3
467	18·2	
500	(20·0)	24·0
516	21·2	
600	(26·0)	29·2
689	32·9	
700	(34·0)	34·4
800	(40·0)	39·6
862	44·8	
1,000	(54·0)	49·7
1,035	56·7	
1,381	75·1	
1,500	(79·0)	73·5
1,728	85·0	
2,000	(90·0)	89·7
2,074	90·6	
2,766	94·8	
3,000	(96·0)	96·9
3,459	96·6	
5,000	(98·0)	99·0
5,190	98·4	
6,921	99·0	
10,000		99·8
10,383	99·5	

(Figures in brackets are interpolated and rounded to nearest per cent.)

The main point to notice is that these distributions appear to intersect at incomes of about £800 and £2,000. This means that the proportion of taxpayers in each of the ranges £0–800, £800–£2,000 and £2,000+ (measured in 1969 income equivalents) hardly changed between 1949 and 1969, but it is also clear that within these ranges:

(a) £0–800: the proportion of very low incomes was higher in 1969, presumably because of the larger proportion of pensioners in the population;

(b) £800–2,000: the proportion at the upper end of the range was higher in 1969, suggesting a wider dispersion of wage and lower salary incomes;

(c) £2,000+: the proportion of very high incomes was lower in 1969, presumably because of increased skill and opportunities in exploiting loopholes in the definition of taxable income.

It is not possible to infer from this evidence that the distribution has remained sufficiently constant to guarantee maintenance of the 1951–52 tax yield (expressed as a proportion of total personal income) because important demographic factors cannot be properly taken into account and because the split between earned and unearned income within each range is not known. But there is at least little positive evidence that the yield would be substantially different.

The main features of the 1951–52 system, expressed in 1973 income equivalents, are as follows:

	(Nominal)		(Allowing for earned income relief)	
	Threshold	Tax rate Per cent.	Threshold	Tax rate Per cent.
1. Allowances:				
Single	494	—	618	—
Married	854	—	1,068	—
Child	315	—	394	—
2. Reduced rate bands:				
Band 1	225	15.0	281	12.0
Band 2	899	27.5	1,124	22.0
3. Standard rate	—	47.5	—	38.0
4. Maximum earned income relief	8,987	20.0	—	—

	Thresholds	Surtax rate Per cent.	(Surtax and standard rate) Marginal rate Per cent.
5. Surtax	8,987	10.0	57.5
	11,234	12.5	60.0
	13,481	17.5	65.0
	17,974	22.5	70.0
	22,468	27.5	75.0
	26,961	32.5	80.0
	35,948	37.5	85.0
	44,935	42.5	90.0
	53,922	47.5	95.0
	67,402	50.0	97.5

TAX ON SPECIMEN INCOMES: MARRIED PERSONS, ALL INCOME EARNED

1951–52 system applied to 1973 incomes			Actual 1973–74 system		
Gross income £ p.a.	Tax rates Marginal per cent.	Average	Gross income £ p.a.	Tax rates Marginal per cent.	Average
1,070	12.0	0.0	775	30.0	0.0
1,350	22.0	2.5	1,070	30.0	8.3
2,470	38.0	11.4	1,350	30.0	12.7
9,000	57.5	30.7	2,470	30.0	20.6
11,230	60.0	36.0	5,775	40.0	26.0
13,480	65.0	40.0	6,775	45.0	28.0
17,970	70.0	46.3	7,775	50.0	30.2
22,470	75.0	51.0	8,775	55.0	32.5
26,960	80.0	55.0	10,775	60.0	36.7
35,950	85.0	61.3	12,775	65.0	40.3
44,940	90.0	66.0	15,775	70.0	45.0
53,920	95.0	70.0	20,775	75.0	51.0
67,400	97.5	75.0	100,000	7.50	70.0
100,000	97.5	82.3			

Table 7

THE EFFECT OF INCOME TAX ALLOWANCES AND REDUCED RATE BANDS ON WAGE EARNERS WITH 75 PER CENT. AVERAGE EARNINGS IN VARIOUS YEARS

Married couple without children: all income earned

	1938-39	1950-51	1953-54	1956-57	1959-60	1962-63	1963-64	1964-65	1966-67	1967-68	1969-70	1970-71	1971-72
75 per cent. Average Earnings	130	290	360	460	510	610	650	710	790	830	970	1,090	1,205
Personal Allowance	225	225	269	308	308	308	411	411	437	437	482	597	597
Taxable Income[1]	0	23·3	25·6	32·7	39·6	49·1	37·0	41·7	44·8	47·6	49·8	54·7	49·58
Standard Rate on Earned Income (Per cent.)	22	36	35	33	30	30	30	30	32	32	32	32	32
Potential Tax Reduction through Reduced bands[2] ..	20·0	19·18	21·52	12·30	11·05	9·67	5·66	5·22	5·18	5·24	3·31	0·0	0·0
Effective Reduction through Reduced bands[1]	0	5·98	6·53	6·40	7·20	7·66	4·13	4·34	5·18	5·24	3·31	0·0	0·0
Percentage of Income paid in Tax	0	2·40	2·51	4·40	5·89	7·23	7·11	8·32	9·17	10·00	12·77	14·54	15·17

[1] Percentage of 75 per cent. Average Earnings.
[2] Value of Tax Relief expressed as a percentage of 75 per cent. Average Earnings.

Table 8

THE EFFECT OF INCOME TAX ALLOWANCES AND REDUCED RATE BANDS ON WAGE EARNERS WITH AVERAGE EARNINGS IN VARIOUS YEARS

Married couple without children: all income earned

	1938-39	1950-51	1953-54	1956-57	1959-60	1962-63	1963-64	1964-65	1966-67	1967-68	1969-70	1970-71	1971-72
Average Earnings	180	390	465	610	680	810	870	940	1,055	1,110	1,290	1,460	1,610
Personal Allowance	225	225	270	308	308	308	411	411	437	437	482	597	597
Taxable Income[1]	0	42·7	41·8	49·5	54·7	61·8	52·7	56·3	58·6	60·8	62·2	59·0	62·8
Standard Rate on Earned Incomes (Per cent.) ..	22	36	35	33	30	30	30	30	32	32	32	32	30
Potential Tax Reduction through Reduced bands[2] ..	14·50	14·38	16·14	8·95	8·28	6·97	5·02	4·64	4·15	3·94	2·27	0·0	0·0
Effective Reduction through Reduced bands[1]	0	7·28	9·20	8·00	7·48	6·97	5·02	4·64	4·15	3·94	2·27	0·0	0·0
Percentage of Income paid in Tax	0	6·71	6·25	8·34	9·10	11·77	11·75	13·14	14·65	15·53	17·83	18·93	18·92

[1] Percentage of Average Earnings.
[2] Full value of Tax Relief expressed as percentage of Average Earnings.

Table 9
PERSONAL INCOME TAX AND SURTAX AS PROPORTION
OF G.N.P. 1938 AND 1946–1971

£ millions

Year	G.N.P.	Income Tax[1]	Percentage G.N.P. (1)	Surtax	Percentage G.N.P. (2)	(1)+(2)
1938 ..	5,175	233	4·5	59	1·1	5·60
1946 ..	8,855	992	11·2	75	0·8	12·04
1947 ..	9,458	902	9·4	81	0·9	10·39
1948 ..	10,517	872	9·3	99	0·9	9·23
1949 ..	11,133	886	7·8	110	1·0	8·94
1950 ..	11,747	903	7·6	114	1·0	8·66
1951 ..	12,976	1,037	8·0	125	1·0	8·95
1952 ..	14,035	1,049	7·4	128	0·9	8·39
1953 ..	15,099	1,004	7·5	130	0·9	7·51
1954 ..	15,969	1,104	6·9	132	0·8	7·74
1955 ..	17,033	1,298	7·0	132	0·8	7·80
1956 ..	18,484	1,307	7·1	145	0·8	7·85
1957 ..	19,609	1,443	7·4	159	0·8	8·17
1958 ..	20,479	1,535	7·5	161	0·8	8·28
1959 ..	21,489	1,607	7·5	169	0·8	8·26
1960 ..	22,872	1,813	8·0	178	0·7	8·70
1961 ..	24,472	2,053	8·4	196	0·8	9·19
1962 ..	25,631	2,228	8·6	230	0·9	9·59
1963 ..	27,279	2,336	8·6	174	0·6	9·20
1964 ..	29,474	2,622	8·9	179	0·6	9·50
1965 ..	31,461	3,160	10·0	184	0·6	10·63
1966 ..	33,153	3,523	10·0	210	0·6	10·65
1967 ..	35,032	3,834	10·9	279	0·8	11·74
1968 ..	37,145	4,360	11·7	220	0·6	12·33
1969 ..	39,340	4,963	12·6	240	0·6	13·23
1970 ..	43,100	5,671	13·1	266	0·6	13·77
1971 ..	48,216	6,223	12·9	286	0·6	13·50

[1] Including Profits Tax and Excess Profits Tax paid by Lloyd's underwriters etc. but excluding Capital Gains Tax.

Source: National Income and Expenditure (Blue Book)

5

THE INCOME BURDEN OF CAPITAL TAXES*

THE fundamental criterion for determining whether a particular tax falls on *capital* or on *income*, is not whether it is levied on the one or the other, but whether it is singular (a once-and-for-all-payment) or recurrent. Thus an annual tax on capital is merely a particular species of income tax; even though it is expressed as a percentage of capital value, and not as a percentage of income; while an income tax which is only expected to remain in operation for a short period (such as the additional income taxes levied in war-time, in so far as they are expected to be removed once the war is over) is really a levy on capital, and not on income.[1] On this criterion, death duties represent a tax on capital; for though they are recurrent (in the sense that they have to be paid each time an estate passes by inheritance) the period of this recurrence is very long; the equivalent annual payment is only a small

* Originally published in the *Review of Economic Studies*, Vol. IX (1942). Section III of this paper was prepared at the request of the National Institute of Economic and Social Research, and appeared in *The Burden of Taxation*, by F. Shirras and L. Rostas, published by the Institute. This abridged version omits some detailed tables.

[1] If individuals behaved with the degree of rationality assumed in economic theory, they would charge some proportion of the income tax payable at the present time to capital account, and not to income account. From the point of view of the efficacy of war finance, this practice would no doubt be deplorable. The fact that it is not done (or at any rate not on a scale which purely rational considerations would warrant) can partly be explained by uncertainty as to the duration of the war and the levels of post-war taxation—an uncertainty which enters, in a sense, disproportionately, into consciousness. But it is also, and perhaps mostly, due to sheer inertia: to the fact that once individuals grow accustomed to charge income taxes to income, and to treat as "net income" what the income-tax authorities regard as their net income, it takes a long time to make them depart from established practice, especially when every such departure necessitates the conscious weighing of future chances and probabilities which most people prefer to avoid. Thus there can be little doubt that if additional taxes of an equivalent yield had been imposed in the form of a special war-time levy on capital, instead of a rise of the income-tax schedules on investment incomes, the effects on consumption would have been very different; though assuming rational behaviour, they should have been the same.

fraction of the amount payable on a single occasion. They differ moreover from other conceivable taxes on capital—such as a capital levy—in that they are not payable immediately, but at uncertain future periods, when the estate passes by inheritance. The estimate of the burden of these taxes as a percentage of income involves analogous problems to those arising in connection with an immediately payable capital tax—a capital levy—but it is more complicated. It may be helpful, therefore, to consider first what is the burden on income of a capital levy, and then proceed to examine the problem in the case of death duties.

I. THE INCOME BURDEN OF A CAPITAL LEVY

1. It can be assumed that the annual burden of a capital levy from the point of view of the individual whose estate is subjected to it, cannot be less than the reduction of the annual net income of the estate occasioned by the levy. Thus if an individual owns assets whose market value is K and whose annual net income is x, and if the proportion l of the estate is taken away by a levy, we may assume, in the first approximation, that the consequent reduction in annual income is lx[1]. It does not follow, however, that the burden of the capital levy lK will be *equal* to that of a permanent annual tax of the amount lx. For, if instead of the levy, the individual were subjected to an income tax of the amount lx which he expected to pay permanently, he would be better off than if he were subjected to the levy; for his annual net income would suffer an equivalent reduction in the two cases, but in the latter case he would also retain command over assets to the value of lK[2]. This command over assets, since it confers power on its owner to make use of unforeseen opportunities, and also a certain

---

[1] We ignore here the possibility that as a result of a redistribution of assets of different kinds which comprise the estate, annual income may be reduced more or less than in proportion to the reduction of the value of the estate; and we also ignore at this stage that owing to the progression of income taxation, the reduction in *net income* (after payment of income taxes) may be less than in proportion to the reduction in *gross income*.

[2] This is because it is here assumed that the imposition of income tax leaves the market value of assets unchanged—i.e. that it reduces the *net percentage yield* of assets, rather than increases their *gross percentage yield*. If it were assumed that the income tax leaves the net percentage yield unchanged, there would be no difference in the two cases. But the latter assumption is not realistic.

social distinction, is certainly worth something, quite apart from the income it yields; the owner, therefore, if confronted with the choice of paying a levy, or paying an annual tax, will prefer the latter unless the tax exceeds by some definite amount the income-reduction due to the levy. Thus, if we write $i = \dfrac{x}{K}$ for the average yield of capital, lK the amount of capital reduction due to the levy, lKi will be the annual income reduction due to the levy, while lKr will be the annual-income-tax equivalent of the levy (i.e the income tax which will make the owner indifferent as between paying the tax and paying the levy) where $r > i$. In other words, to obtain the annual burden of the capital levy, we must multiply the capital sum collected with a rate of interest that is higher than the average yield of capital.

2. It can be shown, on the other hand, that the income-tax-equivalent of a capital levy, *from the point of view of the State*—assuming that the State is free to vary the size of its indebtedness—is equal to lKz, where z is the rate of interest at which the Government can borrow, on long term. For by imposing a capital levy—whether its proceeds are used to repay existing indebtedness, or as a substitute for current borrowing—the State, by imposing the levy, frees itself from an annual financial obligation equal to that amount.

If we assume that $z = i$, in other words, the rate at which the Government can borrow on long term is equal to the average yield of capital of estates subjected to the levy, the loss to taxpayers will be greater than the gain to the State (both expressed in terms of annual money-value) by the proportion by which r exceeds i. Therefore, if the imposition of the levy was prompted by purely budgetary considerations—as a means of reducing annual taxation in the future, or of preventing an increase in future annual taxation, due to the larger volume of debt outstanding—it would be preferable to borrow (or keep the volume of debt outstanding constant) and keep annual taxation correspondingly larger, than to impose a levy. Thus a capital levy, as a form of taxation, is in a similar category to indirect taxes (as compared to an income tax), in that it causes a loss of satisfaction to taxpayers which is not compensated by the gain of the State, and which could be avoided if alternative forms of taxation were imposed.[1]

3. There are two other considerations which are sometimes raised in connection with discussions on a capital levy, both intending to show that the net gain to the State will be less than the loss of taxpayers, or even that the net gain to the State can be negative. One is based on the assumption that the average yield of capital to those subjected to the levy is higher than the yield of long-term Government obligations, $(i > z)$ so that by depriving the owner of part of his capital, and using the proceeds to repay the debt, the annual amount which the State saves (given the *rates* of income taxation) through the reduction in the Debt, will be less than the loss of money income to the owner of the capital. If A is obliged to sell assets which yielded him 5 per cent. per annum, in order to pay capital levy, and the State uses the proceeds to repay debt which carried interest of 3 per cent, A's loss of money income will clearly exceed the gain of the State by 2 per cent. per annum of the amount collected in the levy. If now the existence of income tax and surtax is taken into account, there is a further loss of tax revenue to the State, which must be deducted in calculating the net gain to the State. This loss of tax revenue, in combination with the discrepancy between i and z, may even cause the *net gain* to the State to be negative, in the sense that the saving in interest payments resulting from the debt-repayment might prove to be less than the loss of tax revenue (at the existing *rates* of taxation) consequent upon the levy. Thus, in terms of our previous example, if A pays over 60 per cent. of his marginal income in taxation, the annual loss of tax revenue will be over 3 per cent. of the amount collected, as against the 3 per cent. which is saved through debt repayment.[2]

[1] This is not intended as an exhaustive discussion of the merits of a capital levy, which should take into account other considerations as well. The main argument in favour of a post-war capital levy for repaying the National Debt is distributional: it makes it possible to fix the burden of the Debt on a particular group of taxpayers, the capitalists, rather than diffuse the burden among income-tax payers in general. (In theory, at any rate, the same result could be secured by a differential income-tax on investment incomes).

[2] This assumes also that the effective rates of income taxation of those paying the capital levy are higher than those who owned the National Debt which was cancelled —otherwise, as will be shown below, there would be an offsetting increase in tax revenue from the latter group.

These last two considerations are not, however, on the same footing as the argument mentioned earlier, in that they do not set up a discrepancy between the net gain of the State and the net loss of the *body of taxpayers as a whole*. The loss of income tax revenue, consequent upon the levy, will make the net gain of the State less than the apparent gain; but it will also make the net loss of the levy-payer less than the apparent loss. If there is a discrepancy between i and z, (the yield of the assets surrendered through the levy, and the yield of Government loans) there will be a difference between the loss of income of levy-payers and the gain of income to the State; but this difference will be precisely offset by the gain of a third group: of those who held the bonds which were repaid. For the assets which were taken over by the State in connection with the levy, or which were sold by their owners for the purpose of paying the levy, are not physically destroyed: they will, in fact, be taken over by those who were put in possession of investible funds through debt-repayment. If the percentage yield of these assets is higher than the percentage yield of Government bonds, the latter group will now receive a higher money income.[1] (In other words, the cancellation of public debt through repayment will cause an increase in the average percentage yield of all capital assets). Unless the real return of the assets is less in the hands of the new owners than in the hands of the old owners (which might be the case if the levy forces the surrender of assets for the management of which the old owners were specially qualified), the net loss of money income following upon the levy, for *capitalists as a whole* must be precisely equal to the net gain of the State—though the levy might bring about incidental redistributions of money income between different groups of capitalists. These last two considerations therefore (i.e. differences between i and z, and the subsequent loss of Government revenue from other taxation), unlike the factor mentioned earlier (the difference between r and i), do not constitute an argument against

---

[1] If the income of this third group of people were taxed at the same rate as that of the capital levy-payers, the net yield of the capital levy to the State could never be negative. The latter view assumes, therefore, not only that the average yield of capital to those subjected to the levy is higher than the yield on Government loans, but also that the levy is so graded, and the ownership of the National Debt is so distributed, as to lead to a net transference of income from heavily-taxed to lightly-taxed groups.

a capital levy as an inferior form of taxation as compared with income tax; though they point to the possibility of certain incidental redistributional effects of the levy, between different groups of capitalists, which—if they were regarded as undesirable—could be taken account of, in a rough way, when the nature and scale of levy payments were determined.

II. THE INCOME-BURDEN OF DEATH DUTIES

1. Death duties are also a charge on capital and to estimate their income-burden involves the same problems of capitalisation (or rather its opposite) as is the case with the capital levy. They differ from the latter, however, in that they are definitely anticipated a long time before the payments are due, and because of this anticipation, affect the estate-owner's income a long time in advance—strictly from the moment when the estate comes into his possession. The case is similar to that of the business man who in calculating his current profit, must take into account that there are charges on his capital—such as a loan—which at some future date (it may be in the distant future) must be met. This analogy is not complete, however, for while the business man (presumably) pays interest on that part of the capital at his command which was lent to him, there is nothing similar to this in the case of death duties; the sum to be paid in death duties is like an interest-free loan for life—a "life-interest", with the difference that the beneficiary has command, during his lifetime, over the capital assets themselves as well as over the income from them. Perhaps the best way of approaching the problem is to say that if an individual owns assets whose value is K, and whose average yield is i, so that his current income is Ki, and if the proportion d of his capital is payable in death duties,[1] that part of his current income represented by Kdi is in the nature of a life interest only;[2] a further part, $(K - Kd)\ di$, is in the nature of a life interest for the present owner *and* his immediate successor, and so on.[3]

[1] For simplicity, we assume at this stage that the death duties payable are a uniform proportion of capital.
[2] Remembering, of course, that it is a specially favourable sort of life interest—where the principal, as well as the interest, is at the disposal of the beneficiary.
[3] These formulae assume, of course, that the present owner (and also his successors) maintains capital constant over lifetime. If he increases it by saving out of income, or

The problem of finding the present income-burden of future death duties payable then presents itself as one of translating these series of "life annuities" into their permanent income equivalent. The difference between the width of the annuity-stream and the width of a permanent income-stream which has the same value to the owner (i.e. which makes him indifferent as between one or the other) is the income-burden of the anticipated death duty payments.

2. That there is such a difference is best shown by applying to this problem the same kind of test which we applied for determining the income-burden of a capital levy. Supposing that the owners of estates were confronted with the choice of compounding all future death duty liabilities by paying a permanent annual tax (additional to other annual taxes to which they are liable), it is clear that there is *some* positive reduction of income which they would prefer to accept rather than leave their estates liable to inheritances taxes. The amount of this reduction may vary greatly between individuals (with estates of the same size); but as against the equivalent annual tax in the case of a capital levy, it is likely to be small. For unlike the capital levy, death duties do not imply any surrender of capital, or of income, in the lifetime of the individual; events occurring after death (and even more, those occurring after two or three generations) are likely to be heavily discounted (more heavily, perhaps, than discounting at ordinary interest rates would warrant) in the estimation of the typical human being. Thus it is quite possible that the sum of these equivalent annual taxes, of all individuals owning estates subject to death duties, would be less than the average receipts from death duties of the State over long periods (or more precisely: that the present discounted value of these equivalent annual taxes should be less than the present discounted value of future revenue from from death duties), in which case death duties represent a form of collecting revenue that is superior to income tax—by much the same test by which a capital levy, or taxes on particular commodities, were found inferior to it.

---

reduces it by dissaving, the amount payable in death duties will be greater or less than Kd (and *mutatis mutandis* for the successors). But provided he has a definite life expectation, and expects to save, or dissave, at a certain rate, similar formulae can be worked out for other, more complicated, cases.

3. We have found that the concept of the "income-burden" of inheritance taxes can be given a clear and definite meaning; it is that annual tax on income which gives the owners of the estates the same loss of satisfaction as the future liability for death duties. This can also be expressed by saying that there is *some* rate of interest by means of which the anticipated death duty payments can be converted into a perpetual annual payment of equal significance to the owner—by discounting the future payments down to the present, and multiplying this discounted value by that rate of interest. What this rate of interest is, cannot, however, be directly inferred from statistically observable data—any more than is the case with the income-tax-equivalent of a capital levy, or with the equivalent income tax corresponding to any given sum raised by commodity taxation. It is one of those things which can only be discovered by knowing the individual's "indifference curves". It might indeed be argued that since an individual is supposed to distribute his consumption over time in such a way as to equate the marginal rate of time preference to the market rate of interest, it is this "market rate" which should be used in discounting future payments into their equivalent in terms of present capital value, and in converting present capital value into an annual flow. But there is really no necessity why the results reached in this way should be identical with that obtained (theoretically) by our first test. For one thing, recent work on the theory of saving has cast doubt on the proposition that the individual's marginal rate of time preference, and the market rate, are equal;[1] but even if the proposition were true (and the "market rate" were something entirely unambiguous and tangible, which it is not) it is only when discounting payments (or receipts) anticipated in the *near future*, that we could rely on it. There is no necessity why the psychological rate of discount applicable for long periods should be identical with that applying to short periods; and it is with the problem of discounting over relatively long periods that we are concerned here.

Unless one gives up the attempt to form some quantitative estimate of the actual burden of death duties as a proportion of

---

[1] Cf. Pigou, *Employment and Equilibrium*, (London 1941) p. 126.

income altogether, it is imperative, however, that *some* rate of interest should be chosen for converting the future loss of income consequent upon death duties, or the future death duty payments, into the equivalent in terms of an annual tax on present income; and for the purposes of the estimate which is given below, it was decided to employ the "average yield of capital"—i.e. the rate of interest which emerges by dividing the estate owner's "statutory income", by the market value of his assets (as assessed for death duty purposes).[1] In the light of the considerations above, this must be considered arbitrary; but the choice of any other rate would have been even more arbitrary; this element of arbitrariness is in the nature of the problem and cannot be eliminated whatever method of calculation is chosen.[2]

III. A QUANTITATIVE ESTIMATE OF THE ANNUAL BURDEN OF DEATH DUTIES IN GREAT BRITAIN

1. It follows from the argument of the previous section that the annual burden of death duties is a sum standing in the same proportion to the present annual net income as the present discounted value of all future death duties payable bears to the present value of the total estate. This formula, however, requires some modification when account is taken of the existence of income tax and surtax. In so far as the payment of death duties reduces the size of the estate, it also relieves the estate from some of the taxes which would otherwise be payable in the form of income tax and surtax. The present discounted value which is relevant for calculating the net burden of death duties is not, therefore, the discounted value of the future death duties as such, but the *difference caused by death duties in the discounted value of all future tax payments*; in other words, the difference between (*a*) the discounted value of all future payments on account of income tax, surtax, and the death duties; and (*b*) the discounted value of

---

[1] In 1937–38 this rate was around 4 per cent. on the average.

[2] If a higher rate of interest had been chosen, this would have made the amount of the annual burden, in any given case, less, for the reduction in terms of present discounted value, due to discounting future payments at a higher rate, would have more than compensated for the higher income-loss corresponding to any given magnitude of this discounted value.

the income tax and surtax that would have to be paid in the future if there were no death duties to be paid. It is the ratio which this difference bears to the total value of the estate which determines the proportion of net income which should be allocated to death duties.

Looked at in another way, the burden of death duties is the net reduction of the income-stream of an estate occasioned by it. This is shown, as a proportion of current net income, by comparing the discounted value of the expected net income-stream of an estate when there are no death duties, with the discounted value of the net income-stream when future net income is reduced by successive death-duty payments. The proportion by which the second of these discounted values falls short of the first is the proportion of current net income which should be allocated to death duties. These two ways of approach must yield identical results if the rate of interest employed in discounting is the same as that which relates the income of the estate to the capital.

2. It follows from these considerations that the annual burden of death duties on present income can only be determined if definite assumptions are made not only as to the future rates of taxation (the future rates of income tax and surtax as well as the future rate of death duties payable) and the future rates of interest; but also as regards the changes in the *size* of the estate in the lifetime of each generation, i.e. the rate of saving or dis-saving, both present and future. The burden of death duties as a proportion of income will be all the greater, the greater the proportion of the income devoted to saving. Thus, if an estate owner consumes the whole of his capital in his lifetime—by exchanging his capital for a life annuity, for instance—the estate escapes the payment of death duties altogether; while if the estate-owner in each generation "saves up" for death duties—so that the estate is passed on intact despite the payment of death duties—the actual amount of death duties to be paid, and thus the annual burden as a proportion of income, will be greater, and in some categories of estates much greater, than if the size of the estate is allowed to be depleted by the payment of death duties in each successive generation.

3. The "insurance method", which was adopted by the

Colwyn Committee,[1] really amounts to a special case of our general formula, given above. If it is assumed that the owner in each generation saves an annual sum, the accumulated value of which is just sufficient to allow the estate to pass intact to his successor—or, what (subject to a qualification made in paragraph 7 below) amounts to the same thing, if he takes out a life-insurance policy which is sufficient to cover the total amount of death duties payable, including the increase in the duty due to the policy, and if he does not save otherwise—the net addition to the discounted value of all taxes payable caused by death duties is just equal to the discounted value of the death duties paid (since, in this case, there is no reduction in capital in successive generations, hence no reduction, consequent upon death duties, in the payments of income tax and surtax); and the annual burden of death duties (if the rate of interest used in discounting is the same as the one at which the savings are accumulated) is just equal to the annual savings. In this case, therefore, but only in this case, the annual burden of death duties can alternatively be looked upon either as the interest on the discounted value of *net* death-duty payments or the annual savings, made out of income, which provide a "special fund" out of which death duties are paid.

It will be readily seen, however, that by "saving up" for death duties estate-owners make the estate liable to much heavier payments of death duties than would be the case if they did not save up for it. This is partly because the size of the estate is increased by the accumulated savings; partly also because the more distant death-duty payments, made by successive heirs to the estate, will be on a *constant amount of capital*, instead of on a diminishing amount. The annual burden of death duties, as calculated by the "insurance method", cannot therefore be regarded as *the* burden of death duties, applicable in all cases; or, rather, it is only applicable in those cases where estate-owners do, in fact, save up a sufficient amount to leave their property intact to their successors. It is unlikely that this is the usual practice, especially for the larger estates.

---

[1] Cf. Barna, "Death Duties in Terms of an Annual Tax", *Review of Economic Studies*, November, 1941, pp. 28 et. seq., for an account of the methods adopted in previous enquiries.

4. For certain categories of property-owners it may well be the case that savings made during lifetime are sufficient, or more than sufficient, to cover the payment of death duties on inheritance.[1] In those cases, the insurance method, if properly calculated,[2] gives the correct approximation of the true burden. But in the case of estates beyond a certain critical size—this critical size was the estate of £331,000 with the tax system of 1937–38, and of £86,000 with the tax system of 1941–42—it would be futile for estate-owners to save up for the *full* amount of the death duties, for this policy would leave the estate with a smaller *permanent* net income (after paying income tax and surtax) than would be obtained if estate-owners saved less.[3] For still larger estates, it would be impossible to save up for the full amount; and here the assumptions of the insurance method yield nonsensical results. For these estates—which were estates of more than £1,073,000 in 1937–38 and of more than £190,000 in 1941–42—the necessary annual insurance premium, together with income tax and surtax, would amount to more than the total income of the estate, so that the insurance premia could only be paid out of capital (with the result that at death the size of the estate, and hence the death duties to be paid, would be smaller than the amount on the basis of which the insurance premia were calculated).[4] Thus the insurance method is a *sensible* method of calculating the burden only for estates *below a certain size*; and it is the *correct* method only

---

[1] The size of the estate might also increase through "capital gains"—unexpected capital appreciation, occurring in the future—but this factor must, of course, be ignored in calculating the burden on *current* income.

[2] Cf. paragraph 6, p. 193 below.

[3] Cf. also p. 195 below.

[4] But quite apatt from this, any method of calculation which suggests that the total burden of direct taxation—income tax, surtax and death duties—amounts to more than 100 per cent of income is clearly misleading, for so long as the sum of income tax and surtax amounts to less than 100 per cent., the existence of death duties cannot make the burden *more* than 100 per cent. of income as long as the rate of death duties is less than 100 per cent. of capital. This becomes obvious when it is remembered that however many times an estate is subjected to death duties, the remaining part of the estate must still have some positive value. Thus, if the estate passed by inheritance n times, the $(n+1)$th heir would still derive some positive income from it, however large is n. The *present* net income from the estate, after allowing for taxation, must be greater than the net income of the $(n+1)$th heir. Another demonstration of the absurdity of the insurance method when applied to very large incomes can be derived from the reflection that it asks us to believe that the higher is gross income the lower is net income (net after income tax, surtax and death duties). If it were really true that beyond a certain point, net income decreases with the size of the estate, estate owners would enrich themselves by abandoning their superfluous capital.

if the typical estate-owners in those categories do, in fact, behave in the manner assumed, and save up during lifetime, either by insurance, or in some other way, an amount sufficient to cover death duties.

5. Mr. T. Barna[1] put forward a method for measuring the annual burden of death duties which is different both from the insurance method adopted by the Colwyn Committee and the one adopted in the present inquiry. His method consists of converting death duties into an equivalent annual tax by multiplying an estate-owner's *potential death duties* (i.e. the death duties for which his estate would be liable if he died now), by the probability of death within the current year—his "rate of risk". This probability, and hence the annual burden of death duties on this method, varies of course with the age of the estate owner; but since it is possible to calculate the typical age of estate owners in any particular capital-group, we can derive the relevant annual tax, for each income-and-capital-category, by multiplying potential death duties by the mortality rates typical for the group.

An alternative way of describing Mr. Barna's method is to say that the annual burden of death duties, on his definition, is equal to the insurance premium an estate owner would have to pay in order to insure against the risk of dying, and the consequent death duty liabilities, *in the current year*. His method, therefore, amounts to assuming an alternative form of insurance against death duties —an annual, instead of a whole life insurance—and if the rate of interest at which the insurance company accumulates life insurance premiums is the same as the one that is relevant to the estate-owner's own savings, the discounted value of the series of insurance premiums which the estate owner can expect to pay during his lifetime under Mr. Barna's method (by paying out an annual insurance, year by year, until his death) should be the same as the discounted value of the sum of the life-insurance premiums, for a policy of equal value. (The amount payable *annually* will not be the same, of course, with the two methods: with the whole life method, it will be a constant annual amount; with Mr. Barna's method, it will be lower than the former in the

[1] *Review of Economic Studies*, November 1941.

early years and higher in late years of life). Mr. Barna's method is subject, therefore, to the same kind of objection as the insurance method of the Colwyn Committee: it is not applicable to *all* estate-owners, but only to those who save up a sufficient amount over their lifetime to pass their estates (*net* of death duties) intact to their successors. For the higher categories of estates this is not only an unlikely, but an impossible assumption.

6. The particular form of the insurance method adopted by the Colwyn Committee suffers, moreover, from another defect: it was there assumed that estate-owners take out an insurance policy at the age of 45. The age at which the policy is taken out cannot, however, be arbitrarily chosen; since the purpose of the calculation is to provide the equivalent of a constant annual burden, the age assumed for taking out the life-insurance policy must be such as to provide an expectation of life which corresponds to the average length of a generation, i.e. the average interval of time during which the estate remains in the possession of a single owner. With the present life expectation, the Colwyn Committee's assumption of the age of 45 for taking out a policy implies an average length of generation of 25·5 years. The average length of a generation is, however, about 31 years.[1] Hence the right assumption is for this method that the policy is taken out at the age of 38, since this gives an expectation of life of 31 years.

Calculations prior to the Colwyn Committee's—such as one

---

[1] Mr Barna calculated this figure by the following method. Assuming that the line of succession is from father to son and that the son is expected to die at the same age as the father, the length of a generation, i.e. the period which elapses from the time the son inherits his father's estate until his death, equals the age of the father when his son was born.

From preliminary data of the Bristol survey the following can be extracted (E. Grebenik, *Journal of the Royal Statistical Society*, 1940, p. 306):

In the highest occupational group the average age of mothers at the birth of their first child was 27·95, second child 30·50, third child 31·91; on the average 29·64 years.

Usually the first son inherits. The age of mother when the first son is born is the average between the age when the first child and when the second child is born, which in Bristol was 29·23 years. But as not all first sons live long enough to inherit we ought to take a figure somewhere between the age when the first son is born and the age when the average child is born.

In 1910–15, which can be considered as the relevant period for our purpose, the difference between the mean ages of bachelors and spinsters who were married was 1·9 years, the men being older (*Registrar General's Statistical Review of England and Wales* 1937, Part II, p. 65. Mean age of bachelors marrying spinsters 27·2, of spinsters marrying bachelors 25·3 years). Hence the average age of fathers when their son who inherits is born was between 31·1 and 31·5 years. Therefore the length of generation is estimated to be 31 years.

given by the Chancellor of the Exchequer in answer to a Parliamentary question in 1918[1] and Sir Herbert Samuel's in 1919[2]—assumed the age of 40, which might well have been the right figure for that period, since it is likely that the age at which parents beget children has risen somewhat in the meantime.

7. It follows from what has been said above, that the correct approximation for assessing the annual burden of death duties can only be obtained by taking into account the *expected* increment in the size of the estates between inheritance and death, as inferred from the actual rate of savings in the various income groups.[3] Unfortunately, however, there are no data available for the distribution of personal savings in various income categories. The only possible way of proceeding therefore appeared to be to work out the burden of death duties for *two special cases*, which may be looked upon as the limits within which the actual burden, in the great majority of cases, is likely to fall.[4] The estimates of burden thus derived can, with some looseness of language, be called the Minimum Burden and the Maximum Burden.

Assumption I, that of the Minimum Burden, is that the estate-owners of the present, and every successive generation, maintain their capital constant during lifetime (i.e. that there is *zero net saving* during the lifetime of each generation), so that the value of the estate inherited by the nth heir[5] is equal to the estate inherited

---

[1] Cf. *H. C. Debates*, 11 July, 1918, 108, 53, p. 511.

[2] Cf. "The taxation of the various classes of the people", *J.R.S.S.*, 1919.

[3] Just as in the case of indirect taxes, the actual burden is calculated on the basis of the *actual consumption* of the taxed articles (without taking into account how much this consumption is itself altered by the existence of the tax), in the case of death duties, the calculation of the burden must be based on the actual distribution of income between consumption and saving—i.e. by taking into account just that increment in the size of the estate which results from this rate of saving—since it can be presumed that, in deciding how much to save, estate-owners take the existence of death duties into account along with all the other factors (such as the rate of interest) which are relevant to their decisions.

[4] These two special cases are not true "limiting cases" in the sense that the burden cannot lie outside them *under any circumstances*. The *true minimum burden* of death duties would be reached under the assumption that the estate-owner consumes all his capital in his lifetime; in this case the burden of death duties is nil. The *true maximum burden* would be obtained if we assume that the owner of the estate, in each generation, saves up the whole of his "free income", i.e. the whole of his income after income tax and surtax have been paid. This gives the maximum possible increment in the size of the estate in the lifetime of each generation. But neither of these cases appeared to us sufficiently typical of real life to warrant its consideration.

[5] It is assumed throughout these estimates that estates pass on to a *single heir*. If they pass on to several heirs, the successive death duties paid will be smaller. On the significance of this assumption, cf. pp. 198–9 below.

by the $(n-1)$th heir minus the death duties paid on his death. Here the amount of death duties to be paid by successive generations will be a diminishing series, since the estate will be smaller on every successive inheritance.

Assumption II, that of the Maximum Burden, is that estate-owners in each generation save out of income an amount sufficient to *maintain the net income of the estate constant over successive generations*, in spite of the payment of death duties, so far as that objective is attainable. Up to a certain capital level—the "critical level"—which, as mentioned earlier, was an estate of £331,000 in 1937–38 and of £86,000 in 1941–42, this assumption implies an annual rate of savings the accumulated value of which is just sufficient to pay the death duties (including the increase in death duties due to the accumulation) and leave the estate intact to the successor; it is identical, therefore, with the assumptions made by the Colwyn Committee. Beyond that critical level, however (i.e. for larger estates) the assumption of maintaining the capital intact would have produced a *smaller* net income than could be obtained on the critical level estate. For the owners of the larger estates it would therefore be pointless, if not impossible, to maintain the capital intact. In fact, for the owners of these estates it would be pointless to save up anything at all for death duties, since by doing so, they cannot prevent the reduction in the size of the estate to the critical level; by saving they merely postpone the time at which the estate is so reduced, at the cost of sacrificing the income from the estate in the intervening period. Saving only becomes worth while after the estate has fallen to this level.

It may be noted that these assumptions make the annual burden of death duties (the Maximum Burden) identical with annual savings for estates which are less than the critical size and more than the annual savings for estates which are greater.

It was assumed that savings take either the form of direct accumulation (at the same gross rate of interest which relates the income to the capital of the estate) or else the form of life-insurance premiums, whichever secures the higher net income. For the lowest categories of income, which are not subject to income tax, or else pay income tax at a reduced rate, direct accumulation yields the lower burden, for the reason that the income from investments of insurance companies is subject to income tax, and insurance premiums carry therefore a lower rate of interest. For higher categories of incomes savings in the form of life insurance yield a higher net income, largely owing to the income tax rebates which are allowable on insurance premiums but not on other forms of saving.

The detailed calculations to arrive at the net annual burden of death duties, expressed as a percentage of investment income in 1937–38 and 1941–42, on the two assumptions (I Minimum Burden and II Maximum Burden) are not reproduced here.[1] The results of these calculations are, however, set out in the Table opposite, alongside the relative figures for income tax and surtax in the years and the total net annual burden of direct taxes on investment income: the sum of these two components on the contrasted assumptions about saving to provide for death duties.

The figures illustrate the additional burden arising from saving to make provision for death duties up to the critical level referred to above (beyond which such provision would be non-sensical) for estates of different sizes. They also illustrate the importance, in making comparisons between different years, of considering the total burden of direct taxes rather than the net annual burden of death duties in isolation. The reduction in the burden of net death duties between 1937–38 and 1941–42 (a period during which rates of death duties rose) was due to the effect of increases in other forms of direct taxation.

8. Throughout these calculations, which were prepared by Mr. T. Barna, the following assumptions were made:

(i) The average yield of capital was assumed to be 4 per cent both for 1937–38 and 1941–42. The Colwyn Committee assumed an average yield of 5 per cent, but this was considered too high for recent years.

(ii) The length of a generation was assumed to be 31 years, and the death duties payable in the first instance were discounted 31 years, those in the second instance 62 years, and so on. It might be

---

[1] These can be found in the original version of this paper, published in *The Review of Economic Studies*, Vol. IX, pp. 152–54, along with a note on minor duties (legacy and succession), a table giving the rates of death duties in the two years and a table estimating the burden of death duties using the insurance method (pp. 155–57), also here omitted.

Table

THE TOTAL BURDEN OF DIRECT TAXES ON INVESTMENT INCOMES

(Husband, wife and two dependent children)

Investment income £	Equivalent estate £	Income and surtax %	Annual net burden of death duties		Total burden	
			Assumption I %	Assumption II %	Assumption I %	Assumption II %
			1937–38			
100	2,500	—	2.06	2.06	2.00	2.06
150	3,750	—	2.00	2.06	2.00	2.06
200	5,000	—	2.00	2.50	2.00	2.50
250	6,250	—	2.39	2.50	2.39	2.50
300	7,500	—	2.39	2.66	2.39	2.66
350	8,750	1.19	2.20	2.66	3.39	3.85
500	12,500	5.50	2.00	4.09	7.50	9.59
1,000	25,000	15.25	3.24	6.76	18.49	22.01
2,000	50,000	20.13	4.67	11.00	24.80	31.13
2,500	62,500	22.20	4.94	12.60	27.14	34.80
5,000	125,000	29.78	5.39	17.99	35.17	47.77
10,000	250,000	39.22	5.18	24.64	44.40	63.86
20,000	500,000	47.92	5.33	20.48	53.25	68.40
50,000	1,250,000	56.72	5.43	11.77	62.15	68.49
			1941–42			
100	2,500	—	2.00	2.06	2.00	2.06
150	3,750	—	2.00	2.06	2.00	2.06
200	5,000	—	2.00	2.50	2.00	2.50
250	6,250	1.30	1.01	2.93	3.31	4.23
300	7,500	6.50	1.62	2.93	8.12	9.43
350	8,750	10.21	1.62	2.93	11.83	13.14
500	12,500	20.23	1.60	4.67	21.83	24.90
1,000	25,000	35.11	2.60	7.84	37.71	42.95
2,000	50,000	42.56	3.60	14.03	46.16	56.59
2,500	62,500	46.05	3.59	16.56	49.64	62.61
5,000	125,000	56.64	3.14	14.86	59.78	71.50
10,000	250,000	68.57	2.61	8.57	71.18	77.14
20,000	500,000	80.85	1.15	4.37	82.00	85.22
50,000	1,250,000	90.84	0.51	2.16	91.35	93.00

objected that since all the estates in existence at a particular moment will become liable for death duties over a period which, on the average, is only 15·5 years (since, on the average, present estate-owners must already have been in possession of their estates for a period equal to half the length of a generation), the death duties payable *in the first instance* should only be discounted for 15·5 years, and not 31 years. It must be remembered, however, that the purpose of the calculation is to provide the equivalent of a constant annual burden of death duties; if the death duties payable in the first instance had been discounted only for 15·5 years, this would have implied the assumption that there had been no burden on account of death duties on the income from the estates during the first half of the generation.

(iii) The average yield of capital, the rates of income tax, surtax and death duties were assumed to be the same for all future years as they actually were in the particular years for which the calculations were made. This, of course, is a much more realistic assumption for 1937–38 than for 1941–42 (since income tax and surtax can hardly be expected to remain permanently at their war-time level), with the result that the figures for 1937–38 have more claim to be regarded as a true representation of the burden than those for 1941–42.

(iv) Future tax payments and future net income were discounted at the same rate of interest as that assumed for the average yield of capital, i.e. at 4 per cent. This assumption of a single rate of interest, applicable to all income and capital groups, is, of course, arbitrary. It should be borne in mind, however, that the rate of discount only enters into the determination of the annual burden in so far as it affects the *relation* between two capital values (i.e. the relation between the discounted value of net income with or without death duties); and changes in the rate of discount will only affect the figures for the annual burden to a significant extent if they are considerable.

(v) It was assumed that the estate, on each successive occasion, is inherited by a *single heir*. The extent of the error introduced by this assumption is less than might at first be supposed. It can only affect the burden of death duties in terms of present discounted value, and thus on current income, in so far as the death duties paid on the second instance and subsequently are payable at a lower rate. But since the death duties payable in the second instance are discounted for 62 years (and those paid subsequently for 93 years or more) this factor is unlikely to cause a considerable difference to the present discounted value. The discounted value of *all* future tax payments can, of course, be considerably altered, if the estate is broken up after the death of the present owner, since the estate might then become liable to much lower income tax and surtax payments. But this latter factor is irrelevant for the purposes of our calculation, since we were not interested in the discounted value of tax payments as such, but only in the difference caused by the payments of death duties to this discounted value.

(vi) It was assumed that the whole estate is subject to death duties. Actually, some proportion of estates escapes the payment of death duties altogether, since they are passed on, from one generation to the next, by settlements during lifetime. It is impossible to discover statistically what the proportion of settled estates is in the total, and even if data were obtainable, it is questionable whether allowance should be made for them. For the proportion of estates which thus escapes the payment of death duties varies very widely from case to case; the *average* proportion therefore gives very little information of the proportion which is *typical* in the various income groups.

It should be borne in mind, however, that the omission of this factor makes the burden of death duties, in both of the assumed cases, appear *larger* than it is in reality.

6

THE ECONOMICS OF THE SELECTIVE
EMPLOYMENT TAX*

I. INTRODUCTION

THE Selective Employment Tax was introduced by Mr Callaghan, as Chancellor of the Exchequer, in the Budget of May, 1966, which followed upon the General Election of March 1966 at which the Labour Government was returned with a greatly increased majority. The tax imposed on employers in the so-called "service trades" and in construction (comprising 7·5 million workers, or roughly one-third of the total number of employees) was a lump sum tax of 25s a week (or 125p) on men, 12s 6d (or 62½p) on women and boys under 18 and 8s (or 40p) a week on girls under 18. The tax came into force the week beginning 5 September; and the rates were increased in two subsequent Budgets (introduced by Mr Jenkins), with the new rates coming into effect on September 1968 and July 1969. At its highest level, in the latter half of 1969, the tax amounted to around 10 per cent of wages in the service trades.

The method of collection was linked to the payment of employers' contributions which at that time involved "stamping" the insurance card of each employee; the amounts payable under the new tax were added to the amounts payable in insurance contributions for *all* employees, the tax collected from employers in the tax-exempt sectors (i.e. all sectors other than service and construction) being subsequently refunded. In the case of employers in the manufacturing industries, the refund included a small premium in addition.[1]

---

* Not previously published.

[1] The original intention was to make the tax repayment the occasion of a substantial subsidy to employment in manufacturing industries; in the event, this premium

Since this new tax did not form part of the Government's election manifesto it came as a complete surprise, and the initial reaction, as shown by the leading articles in *The Times* and the *Financial Times* on the day after the Budget, was by no means unfavourable. Later on, however, the business community became increasingly hostile to it, which led the Conservative opposition to pledge to abolish it if they were returned to power. The tax was eventually abolished, simultaneously with purchase tax, when the new value-added tax came into force in January 1973.

As I was the principal originator of this tax (as adviser to the Chancellor at the time of its introduction)[1] and as I have never expressed my ideas publicly on this subject, it seems appropriate to give a retrospective account of how the idea of this tax arose, the theoretical considerations regarding its incidence and effects, and the extent to which the actual experience with the tax bore out expectations.

II. THE BACKGROUND TO SET

Though the appearance of SET in the 1966 Budget came as a complete surprise, there was in fact a prolonged period of both academic and political discussion which led up to it. Among theoretical economists it has been recognised since Adam Smith (if not before) that taxes can have good or bad economic effects which are incidental to their main purpose of raising revenue. Marshall, and later Pigou, put forward the idea that it is possible, by a judicious mixture of taxes and subsidies to improve upon the allocation of resources as determined by the market and thereby increase economic welfare. Pigou, through successive editions of the *Economics of Welfare*, put forward an elaborate scheme for the taxation of particular industries subject to "dimini-

---

was a relatively modest one (7s 6d or 37½p a week for adult males), though a more substantial premium confined to the development areas was added a year later. (This was the "regional employment premium", originally 30s or £1·50 a week, which was doubled in 1974 but withdrawn—on the recommendation of the IMF consultants—in the autumn of 1976.)

[1] This has been public knowledge since the appearance of a book by Mr William Davies in 1968, which in turn was based on information supplied to the author by Mr Callaghan after he left the Treasury.

H

shing returns" and the payment of subsidies to industries subject to "increasing returns" (the industries in question were so named on the specific definitions elaborated by the author) but since he gave no indication of how such "industries" are to be recognised in real life, his scheme remained, in the words of Clapham, a set of "empty economic boxes".[1] At an early stage of my career I became enamoured of the idea that in times of unemployment the level of employment could be raised and real national income increased by a subsidy to employers on wages paid by them and financed out of a general surcharge on income tax (or profits tax). Such a scheme would make the effective tax burden on a particular employer (which could be negative) vary inversely with the wage/profit ratio, and so favour employers who gave employment to a large number of workers relatively to the profit earned; it would also give an incentive to all employers to take on more labour.[2]

In the post-war period, Keynesian policies of demand management dealt effectively with unemployment; on the other hand, the balance of payments problem, manifesting itself in a chronic deficiency of exports relatively to imports, loomed very much larger. Since Britain's export performance lagged consistently behind the more successful industrial exporters, there was a growing agitation (mainly by the business community) in favour of a new tax system which (a) relied on taxes which, unlike the income tax or profits tax, can be remitted on exports and imposed on imports, and (b) unlike the existing purchase tax, is spread relatively lightly over a wide field, rather than at heavy rates on a relatively limited range as was the case with the existing purchase tax.[3] It was asserted in particular that the refund of the turnover

[1] *Economic Journal*, December, 1922.

[2] The proposal was first circulated privately in the early months of 1935. (A reference to this is found in Dalton, *Public Finance*, 5th ed., London, 1936, p. 160.) A more thorough analysis of the economics of such a scheme was presented to the New York meeting of the Econometric Society in December 1935, and published in the *Journal of Political Economy* of December 1936. This paper (reprinted in Volume 3 of these Essays) argued the case on orthodox "neo-classical" grounds which I do not find acceptable today. When the idea was revived in the discussions of the 1960s the case was argued on different grounds—as an alternative to currency devaluation.

[3] One of the businessmen's main arguments was that the heavy purchase tax on goods like motor-cars, etc., by holding down domestic demand, put our producers at a disadvantage in relation to producers in other countries whose home market is far more buoyant.

tax at the frontier had the same effect as a direct subsidy on exports and the absence of such a tax put British traders at a comparative disadvantage.[1]

As a result of the agitation, Mr Maudling, who became Chancellor of the Exchequer in 1962, appointed a Special Committee on Turnover Taxation under the chairmanship of Mr Gordon Richardson to which I submitted both written and oral evidence.[2] The Committee reported against the introduction of value-added tax because they failed to discover any evidence that this tax could secure objectives that could not equally be attained by the existing instruments of taxation.

In my memorandum to the Committee, I did, however, in a final section[3] consider the case for introducing a value-added tax (with wide coverage) not in substitution for, but as an addition to, the existing taxes, the proceeds of which would be used for the payment of a general subsidy to enterprises on their wage and salary disbursements. Assuming that the rate of the tax and the rate of the wage subsidy were so fixed as to make the scheme revenue-neutral,[4] the tax would not impose any net burden on the domestic consumer (since the subsidy would cancel the effect of the tax); but, from the point of view of exports and imports, the scheme would have the same effect as that brought about by a general reduction in money wages and salaries of the same rate as that of the subsidy, which in turn is equivalent to that of a devaluation of the currency by an equivalent percentage, on the assumption that the domestic wage and salary levels are un-affected by devaluation.[5]

When the Labour Government was returned to power in October 1964, and the new government firmly decided against

[1] It was, of course, equally true with the U.K. purchase tax that it was imposed on imports and exports were exempt from it. However under the British scheme, the tax was never imposed on exports; under the Continental tax system (e.g. the German turnover tax or the French value-added tax), where the tax was collected at the various stages, the exporter was entitled to a cash refund of all the tax collected earlier.

[2] *A Memorandum on the Value Added Tax*, printed in Volume 3 of these Essays.

[3] *Ibid.*, pp. 291–3.

[4] This would be the case, as I then calculated, when the rate of the (comprehensive) value-added tax was 10 per cent., and the rate of the subsidy on the wage and salary bill of all enterprises was 12·5 per cent.

[5] Since the higher cost of imports due to the tax would be balanced by a lower share of profits in value-added tax on domestic sales, the above scheme would leave the domestic price-level, and hence real wages, largely unaffected, whereas a straight-forward devaluation would raise the share of profits and reduce real wages.

devaluation, there was an immediate interest in official circles in techniques or policies that would serve as a substitute for de-valuation. It is in that context that I recommended a scheme of universal wage-subsidies on the above lines. In the course of discussion in several inter-departmental Committees which con-sidered this scheme along with other proposals, the idea gradually emerged that the best way to give effect to such an incentive scheme was (a) to confine the wage subsidy (or as it came to be called, the employment subsidy) to manufacturing industry only, since from the point of view of the stimulation of exports it is the manufacturing sector which is mainly relevant; (b) if possible, to pay a higher rate of subsidy in the development areas so as to achieve a fuller utilization of labour resources; and finally (c) to finance the scheme, not by a general consumption tax (such as VAT would have been), but by a tax on employment in those service trades which should be capable of releasing labour in response to such a tax,[1] thereby relieving the labour shortage in manufacturing industry.

A scheme on these lines, along with several others, was put before ministers in the autumn of 1965 but as the balance of payments situation gradually eased no further action was taken on it. However, when Mr Callaghan returned to his desk after the 1966 election early in April he was faced with the problem of raising additional revenue in the coming Budget so as to guard against the danger of an excessive pressure of demand developing in the course of the new fiscal year. At the same time in the light of the commitments made before the election, he was reluctant to raise existing taxes, direct or indirect, in the post-election Budget; if he had not made those commitments the Opposition would no doubt have taunted the Government that they wished to get the election over before unavoidable unpopular measures had to be taken.

It was in these circumstances that the revival of the idea of a payroll tax on services, combined with a payroll subsidy on manufacturing, met with a more favourable reception – though more for the purpose of raising additional revenue than as a

[1] This meant the exclusion of all publicly provided services (like health and edu-cation) and most forms of transport.

means of reducing costs in the export trades. The emphasis had shifted from creating a new instrument for improved resource allocation to the creation of a new instrument of taxation: though the feature of the scheme of paying a premium to employers in manufacturing was retained, the size of the premium was relatively small, so that it absorbed only a fraction of the revenue raised from the tax on service employment.

Hence the main justification for the tax as put forward in the White Paper issued with the Budget[1] was that it would improve the structure of the tax system by redressing the balance between services and manufacturing. Services, including distribution, had hitherto been lightly taxed as compared with manufactured products which were subject to excise duties and the purchase tax.[2]

The White Paper did, however, state as a secondary objective that the tax "will have a beneficial longer-term effect by encouraging economy in the use of labour in the service trades, thereby making more labour available for the expansion of manufacturing industry". After showing that only 10·7 per cent. of the labour coming available in the previous five years, through the sectors of declining employment together with the net increase in the labour force, went into manufacturing, while over 80 per cent., went into services of all kinds, including distribution and construction, the White Paper added that "for these reasons the scheme is deliberately designed to assist manufacturing".

The statement of this second objective produced unexpected and virulent reactions from numerous quarters. Some regarded it as evidence of the intrusion of a wholly unjustified "value judgment" according to which the production of goods is regarded as socially more productive or more important than the production of services (a retrogression to long discarded "classical" ideas on "productive" and "unproductive" labour). Others felt

---

[1] Cmnd. 2986, May, 1966.

[2] Looked at in this way, a tax on labour employed in services appeared as an administratively preferable way of improving the balance of taxation as between goods and services, rather than taxes levied on the purchase of various kinds of services as such—as was shown by an estimate made by Customs and Excise, according to which the maximum practicable extension of the purchase tax to miscellaneous kinds of services, such as laundries, entertainment, hairdressers, etc., could only have yielded some £40–60 million, a fraction of the net revenue of £300 m. from SET, and at considerable administrative cost.

that the case for encouraging "economy in the use of labour in manufacturing" was just as strong as for services—so why not put a tax on labour (instead of a subsidy) in the manufacturing sector as well? Yet others thought that since the tax was bound to be passed on in higher prices in the same way as other indirect taxes, the incentive to economise on labour would be minimal—it would be confined to the extent to which the demand for services as such was reduced, *relatively* to the demand for goods, on account of "services" becoming relatively more expensive, and this was not likely to amount to much.

As against that my whole thesis—which I had put forward in various memoranda during the previous two years (these, under present rules, are due to be "released" in 1994 or after) amounted to the proposition that a capitalist market economy tends to "soak up" labour in the service sectors in consequence of the way market forces operate, and this has the effect that the *average* productivity of labour in the economy as a whole will vary inversely with the relative cost of labour in the manufacturing sector as against the service sector. Anything which raises labour costs in services relatively to manufacturing would, on this theory, improve the "welfare" of the economy and *vice versa*, in much the same way as in Pigou's world a selective system of taxes and subsidies as between industries with increasing and decreasing costs would do. In addition it would ease the balance of payments constraint from which the UK economy had been suffering and thereby make it possible to run the economy at a higher rate of demand pressures and thereby attain a higher growth rate.

This thesis depended, like all hypotheses, on a number of assumptions—of which the existence of increasing returns to scale in manufacturing was one, and the prevalence of imperfect competition combined with relatively free entry in the majority of service trades was another. It implied also a certain assymetry in the methods of price formation between these two sectors.

I am bound to admit that my fellow economists, both inside and outside the Government services, showed a total lack of sympathy (or comprehension) towards these views—which does not mean that they were against the tax-subsidy scheme as such, which in the view of many of them could be justified on far more pedestrian grounds by reference to the differing degree of "exposure" of different sectors to international competition.[1] But I cannot recollect a single economist during the years 1964–66 who would have supported the view that a payroll tax on services would not be passed on in higher prices (or else be absorbed in lower profit or in lower wages) but that in the main it would be "paid out of" increased productivity.

Almost from the beginning, SET attracted strong criticism from the employers in the trades affected (many of whom were small traders), and through them by the Conservative opposition, whose spokesman Mr Macleod (the then "Shadow" Chancellor) gave a pledge to abolish the tax when they returned to power. The reasons advanced against the tax were that it was "selective" and hence "discriminatory"; and also that it would be passed on to the consumer in higher prices—arguments incongruous with their general preference for indirect taxes which are subject to these very objections. Judged by the virulence of the opposition of traders (including the Cooperatives, who frankly admitted, however, that they were not able to pass on the tax to the buyers) which became louder each time the tax was raised, and the absence of any comparable outcries on occasions when the existing excise duties or the rates of purchase tax were increased, it became pretty obvious that the true reason for the unpopularity of the tax with the employers was, despite their strong protestation to the contrary, their inability in practice to pass on the tax in the form of higher prices, so that the tax was (partly or wholly) paid—or at any rate *thought to be* paid—out of profits.

The agitation surrounding SET, and the widely differing and sometimes contradictory assertions concerning its effects, made it advisable for the Government to have its effects examined by an impartial inquiry. I recommended this course to the Chancellor in 1967. The Chancellor agreed, and Mr W. B. Reddaway, then Director of the Department of Applied Economics at Cambridge, who had already undertaken an investigation at the request of the Government on the effects of overseas investment, was asked to

---

[1] Thus the external demand for "services"—with the important exception of tourism—was considered to be far less price-elastic than the external demand for goods; also many types of services were analogous to "non-tradeable" goods which did not enter into exports or imports.

undertake this. Before an announcement could be made, Mr Callaghan resigned following devaluation and Mr Roy Jenkins took over as Chancellor. The new Chancellor supported his predecessor and announced the inquiry and its terms of reference in the Budget speech of 1968.

The findings of the first part of this inquiry on the distributive trades were published in 1970[1] The remaining parts were published by the Department itself[2] after the return to power of the Conservatives (who cut short the inquiry by refusing to provide funds for its continuance).

Though these Reports contain an impressive amount of statistics (a great deal of which was obtained in response to questionnaires prepared for the inquiry) the work itself was disappointing (in my view) in that it failed to come to grips with the basic issues concerning the working of the price mechanism under different types of market structure and competitive structure; and in so far as it obtained results contrary to its own expectations, it was not able to assess what significance, if any, was to be attached to these.[3] The Report bypassed the whole issue of whether the distribution of employment between different sectors is in accordance with the Pareto ideal—i.e., a reflection of consumers' preference *only*, or whether it is to be explained on other grounds, such as the efficiency with which the market mechanism operates. Hence the question whether it is possible to improve a community's allocation of resources by the fiscal instrument—by a judicious

---

[1] *Effects of the Selective Employment Tax, First Report, The Distributive Trades*, by W. B. Reddaway, assisted by C. F. Pratten, P. M. Croxford, I. S. O'Donnell, C. H. Fletcher and T. S. Ward of the Department of Applied Economics, University of Cambridge, London, H.M.S.O., 1970.

[2] *Effects of the Selective Employment Tax, Final Report*, Cambridge University Press, 1973.

[3] In the view of Reddaway, the "unpopularity" of SET was "in large measure accounted for by the 'unfortunate consequences' of the 'widespread impression' given by the White Paper that the objective of the tax was to "move people out of the service trades into manufacturing". Reddaway regarded any such aim as ill-conceived, because in his view "the growth of the number of employees in the service trades primarily reflected the *changing pattern of the community's demands* as it became richer" (my italics). He did not investigate whether this tendency was general or whether it operated mainly in slow growing and not in fast growing countries. In the case of Germany, for example, which in terms of real income per head was richer than Britain, and which should have shown therefore a stronger tendency for the relative growth of service employment, this was not the case; the proportion of total employment in "services" was no higher and rose no faster, than in manufacturing. For the period up to 1965, this was equally true of Japan, Italy and Denmark.

selection of taxes and subsidies—was not raised. Nor was there an attempt in the Report to set out various alternative hypotheses about the incidence of employment and payroll taxes under various assumptions concerning the nature of competition and market imperfection in the service industries.[1]

In the following I shall attempt an analysis of this question on the basis of alternative assumptions about market imperfections and price formation. This will involve complex (and partly unresolved) issues concerning the functioning of the price mechanism in a modern capitalist economy.

II. THE THEORY OF TAX SHIFTING UNDER IMPERFECT COMPETITION

The traditional view derived from orthodox theory is that taxes on particular commodities or services can affect prices only through their consequential effect on supply. Taxes on things the supply of which is wholly inelastic (like the "original and indestructible powers of the soil" of Ricardo) cannot be shifted at all. In all other cases the effect of taxes on prices will depend on the relative elasticities of supply and demand. The more elastic the supply and the less elastic the demand, the greater the effect of the tax on price, and *vice versa*. These propositions were to apply equally irrespective of whether the tax was levied on a finished commodity (like VAT on cigarettes) or on some "input item" (like the excise duty on tobacco).

But orthodox theory assumes (explicitly or implicitly) that commodities and services are traded in "perfect markets" under conditions of perfect competition—where each transactor is faced with infinitely elastic demand or supply at the ruling market price which he cannot influence by his actions. Under conditions of imperfect competition—which applies to sellers in the secondary and tertiary sectors of the economy—the reaction-mechanism of the system will be a different one. The sellers are in general the "price-makers"—i.e., they quote a price to the buyer, and a tax on a particular commodity can be added to the price indepen-

[1] One of Reddaway's associates, T. S. Ward, remedied this in a subsequent publication, *The Distribution of Consumer Goods*, D.A.E. Occasional Paper, Cambridge University Press, 1973.

dently of any prior change in the amount demanded and produced; any effect on supply will be consequential on the change
in (tax-inclusive) prices, and not the other way round.

Under conditions of imperfect competition, sellers, in the great
majority of cases, arrive at the price charged by a two-stage
operation: they first calculate the prime costs (or "direct costs")
incurred, which consist of such labour and material costs as
are directly embodied in a particular commodity, and which
could be saved or "avoided" if any particular unit of the commodity was not produced for sale, and secondly, the allowance
for all other expenses (the "overheads" or "unavoidable" costs),
including an allowance for profit, which takes the form of a
percentage addition (sometimes a series of percentage additions)
to the prime cost (which latter, by contrast, is calculated as an
absolute sum—as so much a piece). Overhead cost comprises
both labour and material costs – though the "material costs" in
this case may largely consist of items such as the rental (and rates)
of premises or machinery, depreciation on sunk capital, etc. The
normal presumption is that the gross percentage margin is not
influenced by short-run changes in overhead costs *per unit of sale*.
Thus the gross margin is not normally changed in response to a
change in overhead costs per unit which results from a change in
the volume of transactions—e.g., when overhead costs per unit
are halved as a result of doubling the volume of sales or *vice versa*.
(This proposition, as we shall show, is not universally true in all
circumstances: it will be more true under certain market structures
than others).[1]

---

[1] In cases of oligopoly with price leadership it is quite possible that changes in
overheads, or even a tax levied on profits, have a direct influence on the margin of
profit charged by the price-leader. But even in these cases there is strong empirical
evidence to the effect that changes in overhead cost per unit which occur as a result of
changes in the degree of utilisation of capacity have no influence on price; the margin
chosen reflects the costs, and the required rate of profit, at the "normal" utilisation
capacity. (See R. R. Neild, *Pricing, Employment and the Trade Cycle*, Cambridge University Press, 1963 and Coutts, Godley and Nordhaus, *Industrial Pricing in the U.K.*,
Cambridge University Press, 1978). In other words, price-leaders make no attempt to
recoup through charging a higher price the higher the overhead cost with a lower
utilisation of capacity: to do so would clearly endanger their position as price-leaders,
since the price-followers would be under strong temptation not to follow suit. This
applies *a fortiori* to price-followers who have no real choice in the matter in the absence
of a prior move by the price-leader. (A corollary to this is that an increase in demand
involving lengthening order books and higher capacity utilisation does not normally
cause price-leaders—or followers—to raise prices so as to choke off demand).

Under imperfect competition, two types of market situation exist, which in theoretical jargon go under the names of "oligopoly" and "polypoly". This is meant to convey that the competitive process in markets where sellers are few is different from that in markets where there are many sellers.

To base the distinction on numbers is not quite satisfactory, however, partly because there is no unique way of defining a particular "market" to which the numbers are to be attached, and partly because the important differences in the two types of market behaviour are the result of numerous elements (e.g. the role of buyers' inertia, ignorance, consumer attachment, economies of large-scale production, product specialisation, etc.) of which the size of the individual enterprise or its share in its own particular "market" (however defined) is only one.

In the following, we shall consider the case of "polypoly" first and of "oligopoly" second.

"Polypoly" covers all those situations in which the individual firm is aware that it can within limits increase its sales by selling at a lower price, and *vice versa*, without being conscious of the repercussion of its actions (if any) on the rest of the market. It is conscious, however, of the risks of selling at a price which is too low (because the larger selling volume at the lower price does not compensate him for the lower margin of profit per unit of sale) and also of the opposite risk of charging a price that is too high (because the higher profit per unit of sale does not make up for the loss due to a lower volume of sales). In other words, the firm has a rough idea, based on experience, of a certain elasticity of sales-response to price changes in either direction; and in consequence it knows that there is likely to be a certain margin of profit at which it will fare best over a period (even if this is not necessarily the best price on any particular occasion). For example, if numerous retailers of men's or women's clothing compete on a price basis and their general expectation in the light of experience is that a 1 per cent. cut in the selling price would increase sales by something of the order of 4 per cent. (or four times as much), it would be against their interest to cut the retailers' margin *below* 25 per cent. of the selling price, since at any lower margin their total profits would be smaller even when the consequential increase in sales is fully taken into account.[1] It is possible that if the volume of sales of a particular trader was sufficiently large he would cover his overheads and earn the normal rate of profit on his own capital by charging a margin of only 10 per cent. But *he would never get there*—unless the degree of imperfection of the market (which is determined by factors over which individual traders have little control, such as the degree of inertia of buyers, their comparative indifference to small changes in prices and their reluctance to incur the costs, in time and trouble, to obtain comprehensive information on buying opportunities) was moderate enough for a 1 per cent cut in price to induce an 11 per cent increase in the volume of sales.

If the entry of newcomers into the market is free and un-impeded so that above-normal profits invariably attract new entrants, the return on capital will always tend to be the same, irrespective of the margin of profit on turnover—the number of sellers will so adjust that the difference will be absorbed by an appropriate increase in overhead costs per unit of sale, due to a lower selling volume of the typical trader.[2]

The competitive market mechanism functions in a different manner in the case of "polypoly" from that assumed in the traditional theory of value. The percentage gross margin added to

---

[1] Assuming that the above 4:1 relationship applies equally with respect to increases in prices as well as reductions, it would be just as harmful to fix a margin which is above 25 per cent.

[2] Up to a point a trader who is exposed to shrinking sales due to new entrants will try to "economise" on overheads—by moving to smaller premises, or, in the case of large corporations, by reducing the scope of activities, concentrating sales on fewer markets, etc.—but there is a limit to the extent to which profits can be recouped in this way owing to the diseconomies of small-scale production which inevitably come into play sooner or later. If there were no such limits there would be an indefinite tendency for the size of firms to shrink attended by a corresponding multiplication in the number of sellers, and it is usually assumed that this process is accompanied by a continual reduction in the degree of market imperfection, so that, assuming that this process were not impeded by rising costs, the market would gradually approach perfect competition. The tendency for the elasticity of sales-response to rise with an increase in the number of sellers and the reduction in the scale of operation of the individual seller, may be true in cases where the imperfection of the market results from *objective* factors only, such as spatial differences, or differences in individual tastes and preferences. But it may not be true when they are merely a reflection of factors like buyers' inertia, lack of knowledge, etc., which mean that only a *percentage* of potential gainers respond to any given incentive—for much the same reasons for which a small random sample is likely to exhibit much the same characteristics as a larger sample. In the "pure" polypoly case therefore the elasticity of sales-response to an individual seller can be treated as more or less invariant with respect to the number of sellers or the share of any particular seller in the total "market".

prime costs will depend on the degree of market imperfection alone (in other words, on the elasticity of demand facing the individual seller) and, under conditions of free entry, overhead costs per unit of sale inclusive of "normal" profits will tend to correspond to it, irrespective of the prices of the various inputs which make up overhead costs (or the taxes levied on them). For whatever these prices are, the costs *per unit of sale* will vary with the degree of capacity utilisation, and the latter will tend to be such as to keep the rate of profit earned by the enterprise within some range (or bound) of the competitive norm.[1]

This means that while taxes on items which enter into prime costs are directly passed on—and with an exaggerated effect, since a given percentage addition to prime costs will now represent a higher "cash margin" per unit of sale—taxes on overheads are not passed on in price; instead, they increase the minimum turnover (the so-called "break-even point") at which a firm is capable of earning the normal return on its capital. Hence in consequence of the imposition of the tax the exit of marginal firms (or of the marginal establishments of firms with multiple branches) will be accelerated and the entry of new firms (or establishments) retarded, until the resulting increase in turnover of those who remain in the trade offsets the increase in the cost of overhead inputs on account of the reduction in overhead costs per unit of sale resulting from the higher turnover.

The peculiarity of some of the service trades (like wholesale and retail distribution, certain classes of restaurant, etc.) is that the gross percentage margin is calculated by reference to costs of material *only* (which is the wholesale price of the goods sold in the case of retailers, or the manufacturers' price in the case of wholesalers), so that the only costs which can be regarded as entering into "direct costs" are those which vary in direct proportion to the value of the commodity-inputs. These include, in addition to the purchase cost of the commodities traded, the costs of carrying stocks, which in turn vary with the period of turnover, the rate of interest on bank loans, the bulkiness and the perishability of

---

[1] Unless the sales of the individual firm are infinitely small, the free entry and exit of firms only determines a *range*—the "ceiling" and the "floor"—within which the rate of return will fall.

commodities, etc. But they exclude all other costs, though these range from items traditionally labelled as "overheads", such as the cost of premises, the cost of labour, whether it be general supervisory staff, or the shop assistants, full-time or part-time. Thus in the distributive trades, and maybe in some other service trades, almost the whole of "value-added" takes the form of the gross percentage margin which is calculated by reference to the buying price of the commodities traded, adjusted only for the cost of carrying stocks (or rather for the deviation of such costs from some norm).[1]

This does not mean that the whole of the labour costs of retail or wholesale distribution is a genuine "fixed cost" which does not vary with sales—the fact that part-time or temporary staff are engaged on busy days of the week (such as Saturday) or in the Christmas season clearly shows that this is not the case. But this variable element in the cost of labour is small in relation to the total,[2] so that "marginal labour cost" is well below the average labour cost. This, together with the fact that in the case of shops it is difficult to introduce a differential system of charging between peak and off-peak periods (with the exception of semi-annual clearance sales) makes it difficult to make any additional charge for the variable element in labour cost. Hence for practical reasons, the whole of the wage and salary bill becomes a charge on the gross margins and is treated in the same way as if it were invariant with respect to changes in turnover.

It follows that given the percentage distributive margins— which in the conditions of "polypoly" we are now considering will reflect the typical firm's conception of sales-responsiveness to price-changes—the amount of labour (and other complementary resources) that will be absorbed in distributing goods, as against manufacturing them, will be higher, the lower is the cost of labour in the service trades compared with the manufacturing trades. Whereas a *general* rise in wages will leave the relative

---

[1] The fact that slow-selling items which particular retailers may have to carry—as with certain medicaments in a pharmacy for instance—are charged much higher distributive margins is clearly not due to perceived differences in elasticities of demand but of unusually large carrying costs in proportion to the value of the articles.

[2] It has been calculated that the extra staff engaged in the month of December, expressed as a proportion of the total, is only one quarter of the percentage addition to sales in that month.

prices (or the relative value-added) per head in the two sectors unaffected (since it will raise the "cash margin" available for paying wages in distribution by the same percentage as the rise in wages) a rise in wages in manufacturing relative to the distributive trades will cause employment in distribution to rise relatively to manufacturing, while a rise in relative cost of labour in distribution will have the opposite effect.

Since the service trades consist mostly of small establishments, labour is not as well organised there as in sectors consisting of large-scale enterprises or establishments. A fall in the demand for labour in the economy as a whole is thus likely to lead to lower wages in the service industries relatively to manufacturing, and *vice versa*; since the workers who become unemployed in manufacturing may be willing to take a job at an inferior pay in the service trades until such time as they can get a higher paid job again in the manufacturing sector.[1] This, I think, is the main explanation why productivity (as measured by sales per employee) tends to move cyclically—it falls in times and areas of slack labour demand, and it rises in times of strong demand. The most remarkable evidence for this is that in the 1929–37 period of high unemployment, output per person employed in the distributive trades *decreased* at the rate of 0·6 per cent. per year, despite the fact that total output (the volume of goods distributed) increased by 2·6 per cent. a year. In the post-war full-employment period 1948–69, on the other hand, output per person employed in the distributive trades *increased* at the rate of 1·4 per cent. a year, despite the fact that the annual growth of output at 3 per cent. was only very little higher than in the pre-war period.[2] Even more striking are the short-term cyclical movements of employment and productivity in the distributive trades which show that productivity in distribution moves with the general level of the demand

[1] It has been shown by an analysis of employment records based on a sample of insurance cards that there was a regular net flow of labour in post-war Britain from the service trades to manufacturing in the boom phase and a net flow from manufacturing to services in the slump phase. In the 1970s this mechanism may have ceased to operate, because the fall in employment in manufacturing was very large, while earnings-related unemployment pay and supplementary benefits set a "floor" to the extent to which an excess supply of labour could induce a relative fall in wages in the service trades. (Cf. R. D. Sleeper, "Manpower Deployment and the Selective Employment Tax", *Bulletin of the Oxford Institute of Economics and Statistics*, November 1970.)

[2] Cf. K. D. George, "Productivity in the Distributive Trades", *Bulletin of the Oxford Institute of Economics and Statistics*, May 1969.

for labour—it increases most when manufacturing industry has a cyclical revival which draws labour from distribution, while there is a larger increase in employment and a check to productivity growth in the first year of the down-turn from the peak labour demand. Finally there is a remarkable negative correlation between the level of unemployment in different regions of Britain and of sales per employee and sales per shop in retail distribution.[1] All these findings are consistent with the hypothesis that the distributive trades (and some of the other service trades) act as a "sponge" which absorbs labour released from manufacturing and releases labour in response to an expansion of the demands for labour in manufacturing—through consequential changes in relative wages and/or in the availability of labour (as measured by unfilled vacancies).[2]

It follows from the above analysis that under conditions of "polypoly" a tax on wages or employment imposed in any particular sector or industry will be passed on in prices to a degree depending on the relative importance of labour costs in prime costs and overhead costs respectively. At one extreme where all the labour costs incurred are reckoned as prime costs, the tax will be passed on with an exaggerated effect—since the percentage mark-ups will not be affected by the tax, the increase in price will be proportional to the increase in prime costs per unit of output (which in turn will be all the greater, for a given tax, the higher the proportion of labour costs in total prime cost). At the other extreme where all wage and salary outlay is treated as part of overhead costs, none of the tax will be passed on to prices; the tax will initially be paid out of profits, but ultimately out of the reduction of overhead costs *per unit of sale* due to an increase in the volume of turnover of the average business.

In intermediate cases where the outlay on wages and salaries is reckoned partly as a prime cost and partly as an overhead the effect of the tax on price may be greater or less than the amount

---

[1] See K. D. George, *Productivity in Distribution*, Cambridge University Press, p. 166.
[2] As Professor George's findings also show a close correlation between sales per shop and sales per employee, this is likely to operate through the change in the minimum turnover necessary to prevent a firm (or establishment) from closing down or to attract new ones (as explained above, the two are not identical), i.e. through the encouragement of the inflow of new firms or the exit of old ones, rather than through changes in employees per shop.

paid in tax, depending on whether the proportion of labour costs in prime costs is greater or less than the proportion of labour costs in overhead costs. If the two proportions are the same (suppose, for example, that labour costs amount to two-thirds of both prime and of overhead costs) the rise in price will be such as to recoup the tax and no more: the profits earned will be the same (in money terms) as they were before the tax was imposed. If labour cost figures more prominently in prime costs, the rise in price will be more than sufficient to recoup the tax; in the opposite case it will be less than sufficient. On the assumption, however, that entry is sufficiently free to reduce profits to normal (or, in the opposite case, to raise profits to normal) the final incidence will not fall on profits but rather on the buyer—except in so far as the same process which restores profits to normal induces a consequential increase in productivity.

The above propositions relate to a *selective tax*, imposed on a particular sector only. In the case of a general tax on wages (assuming that it is "revenue-neutral", e.g. that it is imposed in substitution for some other tax) the effect on prices will be the same as that of a general rise in wages of a corresponding percentage.

All this refers to the case of "polypoly" in which each individual seller can be assumed to arrive at his optimal profit margin on his own, so to speak, more or less independently of the others. Though each is conscious of forming part of a competitive market, they do not normally take explicit account of the prices charged by their competitors; nor do they take into account that a particular action on their part concerning prices, discounts, etc., may have repercussions on the sales of others which may involve the latter in countervailing action that nullifies (partly or fully) the gains which their original action was intended to secure. As Chamberlin put it, in a market with a large number of sellers where "consumers' preferences are fairly evenly distributed among the different varieties . . . any adjustment of price or of 'product' by a single producer spreads its influence among so many of his competitors that the impact felt by any one of them would be negligible and does not lead to any readjustment of his own situation".[1]

[1] Chamberlin, *The Theory of Monopolistic Competition*, Cambridge, Mass., 1933, p.83.

I

This is only likely to be a realistic picture when *none* of the sellers is "large" in relation to others; when their costs are more or less the same, and when the imperfection of the market is largely due to factors such as buyers' inertia that affect all sellers equally, so that the different traders' experiences and their expectations concerning the elasticity of sale-response will also tend to be pretty much the same. Under these conditions it is quite possible that the prices charged by different sellers will be fairly uniform, based on the same kind of gross percentage margins, even when these are arrived at independently without any collusion.[1]

In the absence of these conditions (or some of them) the individual producer or seller is conscious of the constraint imposed on him by the prices charged by other sellers—i.e. that he cannot hope to retain his customers unless he can "meet" the price prevailing in the market; and that it would not pay him to go below the market price, since this would cause others to follow suit, in which case the improvement in his sales would not be large enough to compensate for the loss of profit due to price reduction.

In this case his best course is to follow a purely "passive" policy—to sell at the prevailing market price, and to follow this price up or down (within the constraints set by his own costs which sets a "floor" to the price charged) but without initiating a change, upwards or downwards, which could be harmful to him in either event. This is the situation which economists depict in their notion of a "kinked demand curve" facing the individual seller. The "kink" reflects the expectations of asymmetrical reactions to price changes by rivals according as these are upward or downward. If one assumes that the most important concern of every seller is to prevent the erosion of his market share and to enlarge his market if possible, rational behaviour (within a fairly

---

[1] They may also be the same as between wholly separated markets. It has been suggested, for example, that the proportion of the retail price of a shirt absorbed by the retailers' margin is not very different as between a men's wear shop in Calcutta or New York—despite the vast difference in the wages of shop assistants *in terms of shirts* which may be in the ratio of 1 : 20 as between these two cities. But the average number of shirts sold per shop assistant will also show a corresponding difference, so that the rate of profit on the capital employed may not be very different in the two situations. All that is implied by such uniformities is that buyers' inertia is much the same in the two markets—i.e. that the typical seller of shirts reckons on attracting the same percentage addition to customers (assuming for simplicity that each customer buys one shirt) in response to the same percentage reduction in the selling price.

wide band of profit margins) suggests that his rivals will follow suit if he cuts his price, but will leave him out in the cold (by *not* following suit) if he raises his price. Hence the kink in the demand curve. This indicates that a seller expects that if he raises his price the prevailing market price will remain unchanged, but that if he reduces his price there will be a corresponding reduction in the prices charged by other sellers.[1]

However, since the position of the "kink" depends on the market price prevailing, it would be wrong to suggest that the "kink" of the demand curve in any way *determines* the price. The notion explains the *rationale* of the policy of being a "price-follower", but one cannot assume that *all* sellers are price-followers—to assume that is the equivalent to saying that the price is indeterminate.

This problem only arises however when all sellers are identical in all relevant respects (costs, sales, etc.) which is sometimes assumed as an expository device but which is rarely encountered in reality. At any one time competing firms differ from one another, either in respect of size or in respect of costs or both. Normally the ranking of firms in terms of size will not be identical with the ranking in terms of costs—some small firms may be more efficient than some large ones—but in many cases in which firms grow to an exceptional size mainly on account of their superior efficiency they are likely to reinforce that advantage on account of the economies of large-scale production.

Given such differences, price leadership will inevitably emerge either because in the prevailing market situation it confers an important advantage, in which case one or other of the firms best placed for this rôle will strive to acquire it, or, contrariwise, because it involves a disadvantage, in which case there may be one or more firms who will not be able to avoid having this rôle thrust on them by others.

In both cases the price-leader must be a leading firm, or one of

---

[1] In a world of "product differentiation" the terms "market price" or "identical prices" must be understood broadly, so as to allow for all the differences (quality, location, delivery dates, etc.) which may cause buyers to prefer one "product" as against another, if they are sold at the same *nominal* price. It is assumed, however, that there is a normal premium or discount on any particular "product" to take account of such differences, and hence there is a particular pattern of prices at which the price differences are neither greater nor less than are required to compensate for these.

the leading firms, in the market—otherwise its pricing policy could not exert an important influence on the prices charged by others. If the firm is both large and efficient, it will be in a position to secure the "desired" rate of return[1] on its capital at a price lower than its rivals and thus be in a position to force its rivals to sell at a price which, though it may be above that of the price-leader, leaves them with an insufficient profit to maintain their market share in the long run.[2]

The second situation occurs when, in contrast to the first, it is the price followers who are in a position to under-sell the price leader and thereby "cream off" the market—i.e. to ensure a steady market and a full or at least a satisfactory utilization of capacity for themselves. This is likely to happen when the leading producer (or seller) has a dominant share of the market; but its costs are not markedly lower (and might be higher) than those of its smaller rivals. In that situation the best course of action for the large firm is to fix a price which takes into account the fact that it will only be able to garner the residual demand—i.e. that which remains after the price-followers sell their desired volume, as determined by their capacities. As its only alternative is a price war which it is unlikely to win, because it cannot make the price low enough to drive its smaller but more efficient (or equally efficient) competitors from the market, it is forced to accept a situation of selling at a price that is always somewhat higher than its rivals, thereby becoming the "marginal" supplier producing below capacity and being exposed to the full impact of fluctuations in market demand.[3] Since its margin of profit will be less than

[1] On the "desired" rate of return, cf. Adrian Wood, *A Theory of Profits*, Cambridge University Press, 1975, particularly ch. 3. See also pp. 221–2 below.

[2] Given the fact that a certain minimum proportion of the increase in the capital employed must be financed by ploughed-back profits. Cf. p. 221 note 1 below.

[3] This is likely to happen in an industry containing some giant enterprises with a great deal of semi-obsolete plants and which are not particularly well run. It is sometimes suggested that the U.S. steel industry exhibits these characteristics. But it may also happen in cases in which for reasons of the limited availability of natural resources there are only a small number of producers, one of which is much larger in terms of market share than the others and selling a vital commodity for which no easy substitutes are available. This is the case with oil. Until the creation of the OPEC cartel in 1973, the world price of oil was determined by costs of production (including taxes, etc., charged by host governments and the profit margins of the leading international oil companies). Even though "costs of production" were swollen by taxes and levies of various kinds, it was *not* a monopoly price in the sense of being fixed by reference to the elasticity of demand for the commodity. To secure the latter it would have been necessary *either* (1) to create an effective international cartel which strictly limited

those of the low-cost price followers, the latter will be able to expand at a faster rate, and will sooner or later reach a size at which they can become price leaders of the first type—i.e. in a position to force others to weaken their position by selling at too low a price. This second type of situation may not therefore be stable in the long run.[1]

Under conditions of oligopoly the advantage is invariably with those who are able to under-sell the others and "cream off the market" to the extent necessary to keep their plant fully occupied. This ensures a high and steady rate of profit on the capital employed with all its attendant advantages in terms of planning and finance for long-term expansion. In normal cases one would expect these advantages to accrue to the price-leader; in certain circumstances however they may accrue to price-followers, though the latter situation (as we have said) is not likely to be a stable one in the long run.

The price leader who acquires this position by virtue of being the most efficient large producer will normally aim at a profit margin which permits an adequate flow of finance to secure the maximum rate of growth which it regards as consistent with the maintenance of its position as price leader.[2] This is only another

---

the output of each seller so that the total supply approximated that of a single "profit-maximising" monopolist; *or* (2) in the absence of such an output-allocating cartel, to induce the largest producer to fix a price which provides the "umbrella" for all the others, who could then sell their whole output at or slightly below that price, and yet leave the "price-fixer" with a residual demand large enough to secure it a much higher revenue than it had obtained previously. Saudi Arabia fulfilled all these conditions and was therefore the "natural" price-leader deriving very large advantages from this position despite the fact that the whole arrangement depended on its allowing the other OPEC producers to "cream off" the market and thus be shielded from fluctuations in total demand.

[1] This is true on the assumption that the growth of productive capacity is mainly a matter of the rate of increase in the capital employed which is necessarily internally financed, at least partially. In cases like oil where the possible rate of expansion of capacity is mainly a matter of the size of known reserves, or the discovery of new ones, and where the capital necessary for the construction of new wells, etc., is easily obtained from outside sources on the security of the known reserves, it will not hold.

[2] For reasons discussed elsewhere (in "Marginal Productivity and the Macroeconomic Theories of Distribution", *Review of Economic Studies*, 1966, reprinted in Volume 5 of this series. See also p. xvi and p. 21 of the same volume) the greater part of the investment necessary for expansion must come out of ploughed-back profit; external sources of finance can provide a supplement to internal finance, but not a substitute for it. (Cf. also A. Wood, *A Theory of Profits*, Cambridge, 1975, particularly ch. 3 for an analysis of the factors which determine the long-run profit margin of such a firm.) For reasons explained presently I would not regard this analysis as applicable to the "typical" or "representative" firm but only to the successful firms who determine the price to which less successful firms must conform.

way of saying that it will maximize, not current profits in relation
to the current amount of capital employed, but the *rate of growth*
of profits in the long run—which implies also (contrary to what
is sometimes suggested) the adoption of a policy which maximizes
(given correct expectations) the present value of the shareholders'
equity. As against that the profit margins of firms with higher costs
are constrained by the necessity of keeping their prices if not
equal, at least in the neighbourhood of that of the price-leader;
and their investment will not be one that will maximize their
prospects but something less than this, constrained by the availability of finance.[1]

Since the objective of the price-leader is to set a price that will
generate sufficient retained profits for investment, it will aim at a
surplus over *total* costs, and not just a surplus over prime or direct
costs (calculated, as in other cases, with respect to the average or
normal utilization of capacity). Hence any change in overhead
costs which is in excess of the change in prime costs[2] will tend to be
passed on in higher prices (through an adjustment of the gross
margin) including direct taxes on profits. To the extent that the
price-leader raises his price the price-followers can be expected
to follow suit.

In this way, under conditions of oligopoly, a tax on employment
may be passed on in higher prices even though it ranks as a tax on
overhead items. But owing to the fact that in normal cases the
price-leader holds his position by virtue of being the most efficient
firm, his labour costs per unit of output are likely to be considerably below the average. Hence the average or typical firm
who is in the position of a price-follower, will find that it is only
able to recoup a part of its increased costs (of the order, perhaps,
of one half) through higher prices.[3]

---

[1] If all firms were free to fix their profit margin so as to satisfy their investment
needs it would be difficult to explain why some firms make such small profits or even
losses.

[2] Because overhead costs come out of a gross percentage margin, any increase in
prime cost by some given percentage (due, for example, to a rise in wages) automatically provides for higher overhead costs per unit of output by the same percentage.
An adjustment is called for, however, whenever the items which comprise overhead
costs rise in a markedly greater (or markedly lesser) extent than the various items
which make up prime costs.

[3] In the case of one leading firm of retailers, Marks and Spencer, both sales per
employee and sales per square foot of shop-space is known to be over twice the
average.

The general conclusion then is that a tax levied on employment or payrolls in distribution is likely to be passed on partially under conditions of oligopoly, but not at all under conditions of polypoly. It is not possible to say how far the competitive situation in particular areas or branches of the distributive trades approximates an "oligopoly" model more than the "polypoly" model. In both cases the tax is likely to have some employment-reducing or productivity-raising effect; and while these would be smaller in the one case than in the other, in neither case could they be greater than the percentage increase in the cost of hiring labour, caused by the tax.[1]

III SET IN RETROSPECT

The Conservative Party returned to power in the June 1970 elections, and Mr Barber, the Chancellor of the Exchequer of the new Government, announced the withdrawal of the tax in two stages in his Budget of April, 1971. Had the Labour Government been returned to office, there is little doubt that SET would have provided an increasing source of revenue; the experience with the increases in the rates of SET on two successive occasions had shown that, leaving aside the particular group of employers specially affected by the tax, and the amount of "noise" they managed to implant in the media, the tax was by no means

[1] On the basis of the method of estimation employed by the Reddaway enquiry, the actual increase in productivity in retail distribution exceeded in 1970 by 12·6 points, or 8·8 per cent, the level which could have been expected on past trends. (See T. S. Ward, *The Distribution of Consumer Goods*, Cambridge University Press, 1973, p. 20.) Since the tax at its highest was no greater than 10 per cent., and the full effects on productivity could not be expected to come through except after some years, an improvement of this order could not be fully ascribed to the Selective Employment Tax. It must partly have reflected other factors such as the spread of self-service stores—and possibly, the abolition of re-sale price maintenance in 1961. That an appreciable part of the improvement must, however, have been due to SET is shown by the fact that of the cumulative reduction in employment of 310,000 in the distributive trades between 1966 and 1971 (the years during which SET was in operation) 134,000, or 43 per cent., was *reversed* in 1973, the year following the abolition of SET, since which time employment continued on the same level. (Cf. *The Department of Employment Gazette*, various issues.) Most economic forecasting models at present in use in the U.K. include an SET term in the employment equation to explain the deviation in the relationship between employment and output which occurred during the period when the tax was in operation. According to the Treasury model, for example, SET at its peak was responsible for employment being an estimated 400 thousand less than it otherwise would have been. This effect is considered to have been fully removed after the withdrawal of the tax. (H.M. Treasury, *Macroeconomic Model, Technical Manual*, 1978, Section 7.)

unpopular—or rather, it was less unpopular than increases of equivalent yield in other forms of taxation, direct or indirect, would have been. The typical taxpayer who was not an employer of labour directly liable to pay the tax would have found it hard to say in what way he suffered a loss as a result of the introduction of SET.

From an administrative point of view, SET was easy to collect, since it was tied up with the existing system of payments of social insurance contributions. Difficulties were caused with the de-lineation of border-line cases as between "service" and "manu-facturing" establishments, but these were gradually sorted out. On the other hand the claims of special exemption on the grounds of tradition, hardship or national merit—such as charities or the "living theatre"—would no doubt have continued, but were no different in nature from those which continually plague other taxes such as income tax (or VAT for that matter).

Yet in terms of the original purpose for which the tax was mainly conceived—to improve Britain's economic growth by improving the efficiency of resource-allocation—the tax must be adjudged to have been a failure—not because it failed to operate in the expected manner, but because the general economic situation of the country did not conform to the conditions under which major improvements in performance depended on in-creased efficiency in the allocation of labour resources as between the manufacturing sectors and other sectors.

The proposition that a tax on service employments will lead to a redeployment of labour that will raise the economy's growth potential had its origin in the view (advanced in my inaugural lecture in 1966)[1] that the growth of manufacturing output plays a key role in the rate of economic growth of all developed countries, partly because the growth of productivity in the manufacturing sector itself is a function of the rate of growth of that sector, and partly because the non-manufacturing sectors contain a great deal of disguised unemployment. In Britain the excessive amount of labour absorbed in service trades, due to imperfect competition was the important source. Agriculture continued to shed labour, but the numbers remaining on the land were insignificant as

[1] Reprinted in Volume 6 of these Essays.

compared with the numbers employed, e.g. in the distributive trades.[1]

As manufacturing absorbs additional manpower from the other sectors, the output of those sectors will not, in general, be adversely affected, but instead productivity will rise in proportion to the decrease in their manpower. Hence the higher the rate of growth of manufacturing production, the higher will be the rate of productivity growth not only in manufacturing, but also in agriculture and services, and hence in the economy generally; it is for that reason that the growth of manufacturing output is such a key factor in economic growth.[2]

The mechanism which causes labour to be transferred to manufacturing industry in response to demand is the existence of an earnings differential; agriculture and services are relatively low earnings sectors. When the pace of industrial development is above a certain critical level, these earnings differentials will tend to diminish (since both output per worker and wages in the labour-shedding sectors will increase faster than in manufacturing) and at a certain level may be eliminated altogether. If that stage is reached (which I defined as the stage of "economic maturity") the emergence of an excess demand for labour in the manufacturing sector, though it will tend to increase the level of wages in the economy *generally*, will not suffice to create an earnings differential in favour of manufacturing. Hence the growth of manufacturing industry will become constrained owing to inability to recruit sufficient labour.

There were many features of the post-war economic situation

[1] It was noted already by John Stuart Mill that in certain markets competition is a source of waste. "Retail price, the price paid by the actual consumer, seems to feel very slowly and imperfectly the effect of competition; and when competition does exist, it often, instead of lowering prices, merely divides the gain of the high price among a greater number of dealers. Hence it is that, of the price paid by the consumer, so large a proportion is absorbed by retailers . . . It is well known that . . . professional remuneration . . . the fees of physicians, surgeons and barristers, the charges of attorneys are nearly invariable. Not certainly for want of abundant competition in those professions, but because competition operates by diminishing each competitor's chance of fees not by lowering the fees themselves." (*Principles of Political Economy*, 1848. Book II, Chapter IV, §3. See also Mill's evidence before the Select Committee of the House of Commons on the Savings of Middle and Working Classes, *Parliamentary Papers*, 1850, XIX, page 257, question 852).

[2] Much the greater part of the growth rate of fast-growing countries is accounted for by the growth of output per head, and not by the growth in the total numbers in employment. For all these empirical relationships, cf. T. F. Cripps and R. J. Tarling, *Growth in Advanced Capitalist Economies, 1950–1970*, Cambridge University Press, 1973.

in Britain (at any rate up to the late 1960s) which made it appear that this is a reasonable hypothesis to explain Britain's relatively low growth rate both of industrial production and exports.[1] On this hypothesis, the imposition of the tax on employment in services (*a fortiori*, if this tax is combined with a subsidy to employment in manufacturing) appeared as the appropriate instrument for re-establishing the earnings differential in favour of manufacturing that would have enabled the flow of labour from the services to manufacturing to be resumed, and by removing the labour bottleneck would have stepped up the growth rate.

However, between the time SET was enacted in the 1966 Finance Act and the commencement of its operation in September 1966, the Government introduced a severe deflationary package in July, as a result of which a rapid cyclical downturn occurred and the demand for labour in manufacturing began to fall, *before* SET could have any effect on the availability of labour. Manufacturing employment fell considerably—by 338,000 or 3·9 per cent. during 1966–8 (which was a far greater reduction than in comparable earlier cyclical recessions during 1953–66); and it did not recover noticeably as a result of the strong growth in exports in 1969–71 (which was the delayed effect of the devaluation of November 1967). There was a further fall as a result of the deflationary effects of the budgets of 1968, 1969 and 1970. It appears that the severe fiscal measures adopted in a series of Budgets and mini-budgets from August 1967 onwards led to considerable shedding of labour, and there must have been a fundamental change of outlook by employers concerning the recurrence of the chronic labour shortages of earlier periods.

[1] The particular features of the U.K. economy which supported this hypothesis were (1) the situation in the labour market, as shown by very low unemployment levels throughout the post-war period; (2) Britain was the only country where output per head in agriculture was as high as in manufacturing (in all other industrial countries, U.S. included, it was very much lower); (3) the low rate of growth of the labour force, due to low natural rate of growth, and obstacles placed on immigration, particularly from the late 1950s when Commonwealth immigration was also restricted (this latter factor was not present in the other European industrial countries who encouraged the entry of foreign workers, which made a considerable addition to the rates of growth in their labour force) ;(4) a high ratio of (officially notified) unfilled vacancies to the number of unemployed, particularly in key areas from the point of view of exports. However, none of these factors was present in earlier historical phases (such as the 1873–1913 period) when Britain's relative growth performance was at least as bad, if not worse (particularly in relation to Germany and the U.S.), as in the 1945–65 period; and this historical fact should have guarded against the uncritical acceptance of the labour-shortage hypothesis.

The quantitative effects of SET can be summarised by saying (on the basis of figures of the Department of Employment) that following a five-year period 1961–6 during which employment in the trades liable to SET increased by 766,000 (or 2 per cent. a year), in the five years during which SET was in operation, 1966–71, there was a net *fall* of employment by 400,000 or 1 per cent. a year.[1] In the subsequent two years, 1971–3,[2] the whole of this was reversed; employment in SET-paying sectors in 1973 being very nearly identical to its level in 1966. In the subsequent five years, however, the growth of employment was only 270,000 or 0·6 per cent a year (as against 2 per cent a year in the 1961–6 period).

The largest effect of SET was in the distributive trades which employed 36 per cent. of the total number of workers liable to SET in 1966, but accounted for nearly 300,000 or three-quarters of the total reduction in employment between 1966 and 1971. Following the abolition of SET there was an increase of 130,000 in the number of employees between 1971 and 1973—i.e. rather less than one-half of the previous reduction, after which employment remained roughly at the same level in the subsequent five years.

The "productivity raising" effects of SET were thus mainly in the distributive trades, though some of the gain (as compared to previous trends) must, as we have said earlier, have been due to other causes—mainly, I think, the spread of supermarkets and other self-service stores and of cash-and-carry wholesalers. Nevertheless I think it true to say that a considerable part (perhaps one-half or more) of the tax was "paid out of" increased productivity rather than reduced profits per unit of sale or higher prices (in the form of increased gross margins); the incidence on the final consumer must therefore have been small, in comparison with indirect taxes of the ordinary type such as purchase tax or VAT.[3] According to the conclusions of the Reddaway inquiry "the

[1] This is after adjusting the figures for the increase in self-employment by 220,000 which was fully reversed in 1971–3.
[2] SET was abolished in the Budget of April 1971, in two stages, an immediate reduction by one half being followed by the remaining half, simultaneously with the introduction of VAT in 1973.
[3] Some economists argued that for that very reason, SET was not an effective substitute for such taxes, since it did not have the same "consumption repressing"

distributive trades as a whole did not make any recovery from consumers to set against the cost of SET", but owing to their abnormal increase in the volume of sales per person engaged the fall in net profit (attributable to both SET and the ending of RPM) was around one-half of the cost of SET in manufacturing.[1]

The failure of SET was that it was introduced at the wrong time—at the very time when the prolonged post-war period of full employment and of chronic labour shortages was coming to an end and giving way to a period of steadily rising unemployment that could only be temporarily reversed at the cost of severe balance of payments crises, as in the "Barber boom" of 1972–3. Britain's growing international un-competitiveness—which was slowed down but not halted, let alone reversed, by the devaluations of 1967 and during the period of floating after June 1972—combined with the worldwide recession caused by the rise in commodity prices and the fourfold rise in the oil price, caused unemployment to reach pre-World War II levels by 1975; current forecasts (in June 1979) envisage it rising to 2 million within the next year or so.

It is intriguing to speculate how Britain's performance would

---

effect. This however is a mistaken view of the ordinary principles of public finance, according to which the purpose of taxation is to provide sufficient resources for public use by reducing the sum of disposable incomes in relation to the value of production generated by any particular form of economic activity. A given sum extracted in the form of pay-roll tax reduces this ratio in much the same way as other taxes do; the fact that prices do not rise because the value of output per worker has risen (or the cost per unit of labour has fallen) does not make it any the less effective in providing resources for Government purposes. A difference arises only when the main purpose of taxation is looked upon as a reduction of *consumption as such*, and not the provision of resources in a non-inflationary manner. This might be the case, e.g., when the fiscal policy of the Government is governed by a balance of payments constraint (i.e. the need to hold down domestic consumption and investment to a level at which the imports generated do not exceed exports) and not by a resource constraint. In this latter case SET is not an appropriate fiscal instrument—for the same reasons for which productivity increase is of no social benefit unless the labour released thereby can be re-employed elsewhere. It was also contended by some (cf. Mitchell, *British Journal of Industrial Relations*, Nov. 1969) that differences in "skill requirements" between services and manufacturing mean that the labour released in services is not suitable for employment in manufacturing. However, as Sleeper (op. cit.) and others have argued, there are large cyclical flows of labour between services and manufacturing (which are positive in boom years and negative in slump years), and in fact distribution has provided the largest single source of labour for manufacturing in years of economic expansion in the 1959–66 period, and manufacturing was an important alternative source of employment for persons working in distribution. In the event, SET, coming as it did in a period of falling demand for labour in manufacturing, had the effect of inhibiting the re-flux of labour from manufacturing to distribution that would otherwise have taken place. (See Sleeper, op. cit., pp. 293–4.)

[1] Cf. Reddaway, First Report, op. cit., p. 124.

have improved if SET had been introduced in the early 1950s, at a time when manpower shortages (more than physical capacity shortages) set a limit to both investment and exports and when, with the coming of rearmament and the outbreak of the Korean war, the rise in the volume of exports fell to 1–2 per cent. a year (as against the 15 per cent. a year in the period 1947–51).[1]

But with the strong rise of imports of manufactures after the removal of restrictions in the late 1950s, and the slow rise in exports due to falling competitiveness in relation to Japan, Germany and some other countries, Britain was heading towards a chronic labour-surplus situation of the pre-war type, long before the world recession caused by the commodity-price inflation and the oil crisis of the 1970s. Added to this the new technological revolution in automatic control systems (the "silicon chips") now threatens to upset past relationships between the growth of production and employment both in industry and services; it is possible, or even likely, that the maximum permissible rate of growth as governed by energy and raw material availabilities will be combined in future with *falling* labour requirements in both the secondary and tertiary sectors. If that comes about the objective of saving labour and raising productivity through reduced overmanning, etc., will give way to the opposite concern of creating conditions of maximum work-sharing, so as to secure participation in the productive process for the largest number of adults. Clearly it is better to halve productivity than to leave half the working population in a state of listless idleness. In that world, if it materialises, we shall need taxes which lower productivity and not those which raise it.

[1] This was at a time when, following upon the devaluation of 1949, the pound was clearly undervalued—at any rate in relation to the dollar.

A NEW LOOK AT THE EXPENDITURE TAX[1]

THERE has been a revival of interest recently in the idea of replacing personal income tax by a personal expenditure tax. As one who explored the idea more than a quarter of a century ago,[1a] and later had a share in getting it adopted (albeit not very successfully) in India and Ceylon, I feel it incumbent on me to say how far my position on the issue has changed, and how far I subscribe to the various schemes recently advocated on both sides of the Atlantic.[2]

The basic issue of income versus expenditure as the ideal measure of taxable capacity can be discussed at various levels.

To some economists, of whom Irving Fisher is the most famous, the real meaning of income is a flow of personal satisfactions or more accurately that part of it which is derived from the consumption (or destruction) of things which have an exchange value, the sum of which can be expressed in terms of exchange value (or purchasing power).[3] Looked at in this way, the measure of the aggregate flow over a time interval is consumption, and not

---

[1] Based on a talk given at a Brookings Conference on *Income versus Expenditure Taxes* in Washington, October 1978.

[1a] *An Expenditure Tax*, London, Allen and Unwin, 1955.

[2] Cf. J. E. Meade and associates, *The Structure and Reform of Direct Taxation*, Report to the Institute of Fiscal Studies, London, Allen and Unwin, 1978; J. A. Kay and M. A. King, *The British Tax System*, Oxford, 1978; *The Expenditure Tax*, by James Griffin on behalf of the Advisory Commission on Intergovernmental Relations, Washington D.C., 1974; U.S. Department of the Treasury, *Blueprints for Basic Tax Reform*, 1977; William D. Andrews, *A Supplemental Personal Expenditure Tax*, to be published by the Brookings Institution, Washington D.C.; David F. Bradford, *The Case for a Personal Consumption Tax*, ditto; M. J. Graetz, *Implementation of a Progressive Tax on Consumption*, ditto; S. O. Lodin, *Progressive Expenditure Tax—An Alternative?*, Stockholm, 1978.

[3] There are innumerable kinds of satisfactions—such as friendship, divine worship, the contemplation of beautiful objects, love in its various forms, etc.—which cannot be bought and sold and must therefore be left out of account.

what is usually regarded as income, which is consumption plus net saving. According to Fisher, net saving over a period is nothing else but the discounted value of the *increment* to the flow of future satisfactions resulting from decisions made in the current period; and the addition of the discounted value of future satisfactions to the (undiscounted) sum of current satisfactions involves double counting. Saving is an addition to future satisfactions; it should not therefore also be counted as part of present satisfactions as well.

As against that is the Haig-Simons conception of income as "the net increment of economic power between two points of time". Here the basic notion is the addition, over a time interval, to an individual's command over society's scarce resources, irrespective of how much or how little of it he chooses to exercise for the purpose of current consumption.

On the Haig-Simons view it is a man's command over scarce resources which is the measure of his "economic power", and this in turn is the proper yardstick for assessing his capacity to contribute to the expenses of society.

There is no particular virtue, however, in measuring this power by its annual increment rather than its total at a given moment. An annual wealth tax which assesses individuals according to their power of command over resources as such may therefore appear a more reliable measure than an income tax which takes account of the current increment of economic power only.

There are, however, at least two reasons why historically a tax based on income appears the more natural (and reasonable) measure of taxable capacity than a tax based on the sources of income.

One is that "power of command" over resources has different implications according to whether or not a man's wealth consists of things that can be disposed of at a moment's notice, so that he is free to exercise that power at any time—whether for the satisfaction of personal needs or whims, the exploitation of an opportunity to make a profitable investment, or in ways that add to his influence over his fellow men or to the esteem in which he is held. At one extreme is the case where a man keeps the bulk of his wealth in gold or other precious metals or in bank accounts that can be withdrawn on demand or at short notice. It would be universally agreed that the taxable capacity of such individuals cannot be measured by their income, however defined. At the other extreme is the man who holds a life interest in an entailed estate which he cannot dispose of; his true command over resources is confined to the value of the produce of the land. Even if the land is not entailed, the owner of it in a predominantly agricultural community would not regard it as a disposable asset; the actual measure of his command over resources (or his "wealth") is the harvest from the soil, not the soil itself. In a modern capitalist community where physical assets are to a predominant extent "owned" by legal personalities—by companies, public or private—with the corollary that an individual's ownership consists of negotiable titles to wealth, in the form of stocks and shares, the distinction between "disposable" and "non-disposable" wealth is blurred. In this latter case, the annual yield (in the form of interest and dividends) on such "financial assets" may vary for all kinds of reasons as between different "titles" which are in no relation to the relative advantages which their possession confers on the owners. In this case an annual wealth tax may give a far more reliable measure of taxation in accordance with "economic power" than a tax levied on interest and dividends.[1]

A second reason is that the wealth residing in personal earning power—which has no market value because it cannot be alienated, any more than entailed land—cannot, as such, serve as a measure of taxable capacity. Hence in regard to the economic benefits derived from work-performance, there is no alternative to income as a measure of "economic power". On the other hand it is desirable that the taxable capacity derived from material possessions and from personal earning power should be assessed on a comparable basis, particularly since many individuals derive "economic power" from both sources simultaneously and a progressive system requires that incomes from all sources should be aggregated. This can only be accomplished through a personal income tax; though the imposition of a progressive tax on income from all sources does not exclude a supplemental tax on material

---

[1] Though this is less certain in relation to a comprehensive income tax which includes capital gains as income.

wealth, which can be justified on the ground that the possession of disposable assets endows its owners with an additional "economic power" which has no equivalent in the case of those whose sources of income are non-disposable (or inalienable).

As I think I made clear in my book, I found the Haig-Simons conception of taxable capacity intellectually more appealing than the Fisherian conception—except on the ground of social ethics which suggests that it is better to tax people on the basis of what they take out of the common pool than on the basis of what they put into it. However, from the point of view of distributive justice this is not a decisive consideration. I came to the advocacy of an expenditure tax mainly on account of the difficulties of finding a definition of income that gives proper effect to the Haig-Simons conception; and the impossibility, in terms of legislative and administrative practice, of approximating such notion of income for tax purposes, even if a theoretically satisfactory definition were found.

The Haig conception, as Simons has shown,[1] is identical with the sum of consumption and net saving. All the difficulties with income tax concern the problem of taxing "net savings" in a comprehensive manner that is just and fair as between individuals in different circumstances. As Simons so convincingly argued, capital appreciation—an increase in the market value of a man's properties—is a form of saving and no different in nature from an increase in the value of assets of the same magnitude which results from an addition to the stock of assets, such as the purchase of bonds and shares out of current income. Indeed, an appreciation in the value of ordinary shares may be no more than the equivalent of the savings made in the form of retentions by companies on behalf of their shareholders. In an ideal system therefore capital gains should be treated in the same way as other forms of income; moreover, to be just between different taxpayers, capital gains should be taxed as they accrue, and not only when the assets are realised. However, it is generally agreed that the annual taxation of unrealised capital appreciation would be an administrative nightmare. For that reason even the most ardent advocates of a comprehensive income tax stop short of advocating it.

[1] Henry Simons, *Personal Income Taxation* (Chicago, 1938).

But the basic difficulties with the notion of net saving do not lie with the realisation criterion (which involves, in effect, a reduction in the effective rates of taxation as compared with savings made out of "ordinary" income, and one which varies for wholly accidental reasons between different taxpayers) but on the question whether the appreciation in the value of financial assets is in the nature of an *accrual* (which is invariably a *process* in time) or whether it is the result of a re-valuation of future prospects (which normally occurs at a *point* in time). An increase in value which has its counterpart in an increment of assets (i.e. that which enters into "saving" in the sense defined for national income purposes) is clearly in the nature of an *accrual*. But a revaluation of existing assets (which is not part of "saving" as defined for the purposes of national income calculations) can nevertheless be an addition to an individual's "economic power", if it represents an increase in his command over goods and services. In assessing the taxable capacity of different *individuals* the notion of saving cannot be restricted to accruals only—any more than one can say that a business earns a true profit only by making more shoes, not from selling more attractive or fashionable shoes for which it is able to charge a higher price.

However, this is not true of *all* re-valuations, and it is not possible—in theory, let alone as a matter of practical administration—to isolate the genuine kind from the non-genuine kind. If two taxpayers spend equal amounts over the same period, they can be *presumed* to have had the same real consumption—though in times of inflation this statement will only be true within limits, since one person's expenditure-basket may have shown a larger rise in prices (between two points of time) than another person's. Nevertheless the extent of arbitrariness thereby introduced is limited and could be safely disregarded for practical purposes. But when it comes to net saving, two persons who show the same net amount of saving in terms of money—irrespective of whether the saving represents a transfer of funds from an income account to a capital account (i.e. the purchase of additional shares out of income) or merely the appreciation in the value of shares already held—will not normally have gained equally in terms of "economic power". In times of inflation allowances should be made for the reduced purchasing power of money, if only because any given rate of inflation will have differing implications for different taxpayers according to their individual circumstances. Thus when the rate of inflation is, say, 10 per cent. a year and two taxpayers have both made in a particular year a net saving of £100 in terms of money, the net addition to "economic power" would be negative to a person who had £2000 to start with, but positive to the man who started with less than £1000. The appropriate adjustment for inflation is not a simple matter of the indexation of net saving; the proper allowance depends not only on the rise in prices in a given period, but on the relationship of the current accrual of wealth to the volume of a person's possessions at the beginning of the period.[1]

As I have shown in my book, the same kind of problem arises when capital values change owing to a change in the rate of interest (rather than in the expectation of future yields or earnings) and this in turn is analogous to the re-valuation which is the result, not of a change in the rate of interest, but of a change in the (subjective) uncertainty surrounding the expectations of future earnings which are discounted.

I therefore came down in favour of the expenditure tax principle not just because of the loopholes and defects in existing systems of income tax but because of basic limitations of the income concept which make it impossible to give practical effect to the Haig-Simons conception, no matter how the tax laws are framed. In that sense my advocacy of an expenditure tax was that of a second best. If "spending power" is measured by actual spending, there is an injustice in the allocation of the tax burden as between misers and spendthrifts. But if it is assumed (which I

[1] It is for this reason that partial indexation of certain forms of gain (which is the only adjustment that appears practicable) by "writing up" the costs of assets by some price index may create more inequities between taxpayers than would exist without it. It would be unfair to index gains without also indexing losses; to do this adequately would require an annual valuation of *all* assets (including cash, bank deposits, etc.) and not only those which happen to be bought and sold in a particular year. As numerous writers pointed out, so long as inflation persists, the taxation of capital gains (measured in money terms) includes an element of a wealth tax, and serves as some kind of substitute for the latter. The wealth tax element will not be a too large one so long as the yield of the capital gains tax amounts to no more than a small proportion of the value of privately owned wealth. The fact that the tax falls mainly on those whose capital is appreciating most (since there is bound to be a fairly strong correlation, at any rate over a run of years, between capital appreciation and realised capital gains) is thus not necessarily a "distributional evil"—even in times of inflation.

think is not an unreasonable assumption) that different individuals' propensity to spend does not vary much because of differences in tastes and temperaments (as Pigou called it), but mainly because of objective factors that a tax system can make allowance for—for example, the number of dependents—a tax based on actual spending may give a better approximation of true spending power than any practically feasible tax on income.

There is no need, however, to opt for one to the exclusion of the other; and as I argued in a later work,[1] in a society composed of individuals who draw benefits in many forms from widely different sources, a system of personal direct taxation based on a number of criteria (such as income, expenditure, capital gains, net wealth, the receipt of gifts and inheritances) may give a more reasonable or more reliable allocation of taxation in accordance with taxable capacity than a system based on a single criterion only.

Such a "multiple-criteria" system would have two practical advantages. First, it would make it very much easier to operate a personal expenditure tax on a "cash flow" basis—i.e. by the method of measuring expenditure as the difference between cash received from all sources and all non-taxable outlays. (All advocates of a graduated personal expenditure tax, at least from Irving Fisher onwards[2] agree that the only practical way of ascertaining how much a person spent over a period is by taking what a person had at the beginning of the period, adding his cash receipts during the period and subtracting what he was left with at the end, including in the latter the net purchases during the year of capital assets of all kinds.) However this depends on the tax authorities receiving regular and comprehensive information on cash received from all sources—from the sale of assets, from depletion of cash and bank balances, borrowings, business withdrawals, gifts and inheritances, as well as the receipts which rank as "income payments" and are thus liable to tax under present law. Though in principle it would be possible for the tax authorities to request all this information for the purposes of the expenditure tax only (just as is done now when the

---

[1] *Indian Tax Reform, Report of a Survey* (New Delhi, Ministry of Finance, Government of India, 1956), reprinted in Volume 8 of these Essays.

[2] Cf. I. Fisher, "Income in Theory and Income Taxation in Practice", *Econometrica* (1937).

Revenue requires a "wealth statement" in the so-called "back-duty" cases) in practice it is difficult to imagine that all this information would be readily forthcoming, unless the information would be readily forthcoming, unless the information was required for the purposes of assessment of some tax—such as the annual wealth tax, the tax on capital gains (which already involves reporting on the purchases of all capital assets), a gift and inheritance tax, as well as an income tax.[1]

A second advantage of a multiple-based system is that it would make it easier to introduce the expenditure tax, not as a complete replacement of income tax, but as a supplemental tax which would replace the higher rates of income tax (i.e. something corresponding to the old surtax) and not the basic-rate income tax. For reasons given in my book there are important advantages in this procedure, not least of which is that it would make the transitional problems of changing over to the new system less serious than they would be otherwise.[2] Another advantage is that while there are numerous incongruous concessions to savings in the existing tax legislation (in the form of life assurances, super-annuation and mortgage relief, as well as various kinds of subsidies on investment) it is only in the higher ranges of wealth or income that these concessions become really anomalous, since they make it possible for the wealthier taxpayer to claim tax relief on purely fictitious savings which are offset, or more than offset, by dis-savings out of capital or capital gains. The expenditure of the typical wage and salary earner is far more closely geared to his taxable income: hence the exemption of savings in his case (with the exception of mortgage relief) does not make so much difference in the *relative* burden of taxation as between different individuals. Since such savings (mainly contractual) are a relatively small proportion of income, their exemption goes to reduce the yield of any given tax schedule without greatly changing the distribution of taxation between taxpayers. In the higher income ranges, however (and particularly in the case of incomes

[1] As I recommended in my Indian tax report, the liability to all these taxes could be assessed on the basis of information given in a single comprehensive return.

[2] The recent U.S. advocates of an expenditure tax, particularly Professor William D. Andrews, came down in favour of a supplemental tax, and so did the Meade Report. (Cf. his paper "A Supplemental Personal Expenditure Tax" in the forthcoming Brookings publication.)

derived from capital), these various concessions produce highly anomalous results.

What I feel about the recent advocates of the change-over from income to expenditure as the basis of personal taxation—on both sides of the Atlantic—is the same as what I now think about my own writing of twenty-five years ago. They both show a lack of awareness (or at least of sufficient awareness) of the political and sociological problems involved in closing tax loopholes. A highly distorted and loophole-ridden income tax is compared with an expenditure tax drawn up on the right principles and free of distortions and of anomalous concessions resulting from political pressures.

In fact, as the example of India shows, it is just as easy to make a mockery of an expenditure tax as it has been with progressive income tax. The Expenditure Tax Bill, introduced by the Finance Minister, the late T. T. Krishnamachari, in 1957, was so severely mauled in its passage through the Lokh Saba (the Indian Parliament) that the outcome was a joke—incapable of enforcement, and a sheer waste of time for the tax administration. The particular provision which crippled the tax in the case of India was that the liability to the tax was tied to a minimum income limit and not a minimum expenditure limit. All that was necessary to avoid any liability to the expenditure tax was to manipulate income so that the critical limit was not attained at least in those years in which a sizeable expenditure tax liability would have been incurred. And as everyone knows it is not difficult to avoid having an excessive income. In addition the Act contained a long series of exemptions—such as expenditure on marriages, on medical expenses, the purchase of cottage industry products, etc., which have no counterpart in the income tax laws. There is little doubt that if the tax had not been withdrawn fairly soon after its introduction these loopholes would have become wider.[1]

If, as has been argued, "the current political climate is not hospitable to the taxation of capital or an increase in the taxation of capital gains", why is it supposed that it is hospitable to the

[1] For my contemporary views on the Indian tax reform introduced following my recommendations, cf. my paper *Tax Reform in India* originally published in the *Economic Weekly*, Bombay, January 1959, and reprinted in Volume 3 of these Essays.

introduction of a progressive expenditure tax? The very idea of such a tax was *unanimously* rejected by the Finance Committee of the United States Senate, and this was during a particularly critical phase of World War II (in September 1942) with the tax intended for the duration of the war only.

There are, as is well known, many millionaires in the United States, in England and in other countries who manage to avoid payment of income tax—because they can avoid having a *net* taxable income—who yet live in great luxury and manage to become steadily richer as well. It would be easy to conceive of changes in the tax laws that would make these people just as liable to taxation as the man in the street. Since this is not done there must be powerful political reasons for it; and these reasons would be just as powerful whether the attempt to create a genuine system of progressive taxation were made through a supplemental expenditure tax or through a reform of the income tax.[1]

The strongest political argument in favour of a supplemental expenditure tax is that it removes (or at least it greatly weakens) the case which is so frequently made against progressive taxation on the grounds that it reduces the funds available for savings of those taxpayers who, on account of their high incomes, are alone in a position to save a substantial part of their incomes. If net savings are exempt from taxation (or taxed only at a low rate) it cannot be said that the well-to-do are deprived through taxation of the means to save.

However, this argument is not as strong as it appears—not if one believes (as I do) that the market mechanism always generates sufficient profits to finance the investment that entrepreneurs decide to undertake. An expenditure tax, by encouraging savings and discouraging spending of the well-to-do, will not thereby cause more investment to be undertaken unless there are other

[1] Indeed there is a group of American economists who use one of the arguments in favour of the expenditure tax principle—i.e. that it avoids the double taxation of savings—for advocating the abolition of *all* taxes on profit, interest and dividends and turning the existing income tax into a wage tax. The argument is that all capital is the fruit of past saving; it must therefore have suffered taxation *already* when it was first accumulated out of taxed income; and the simplest way to avoid the double taxation of savings is not to exempt net savings when they are made, but to exempt the fruits of savings. Since all extant capital must have been "saved" by someone sometime, this, according to this view, "justifies" exempting all unearned income from taxation altogether (see David Bradford, *The Case for a Personal Consumption Tax*, op. cit.; also *Blueprints for Basic Tax Reform*, Department of the Treasury, Washington D.C., 1977).

incentives (of a monetary or fiscal kind) which ensure that there is more investment *pari passu* with the reduced spending of the well-to-do. But assuming that such instruments are available, and appropriate policies of economic management are followed by the Government, much the same distribution of resources between investment and luxury consumption could be secured (in principle) under the one system as under the other.

INDEX TO AUTHORS